Chief Kickboxing Officer

Chief Kickboxing Officer

Applying the Fight Mentality to Business Success

Alfonso Asensio

BEP BUSINESS EXPERT PRESS

Chief Kickboxing Officer: *Applying the Fight Mentality to Business Success*

First published in 2019 by
Business Expert Press, LLC
222 East 46th Street, New York, NY 10017
www.businessexpertpress.com

ISBN-13: 978-1-94999-144-4 (paperback)
ISBN-13: 978-1-94999-145-1 (e-book)

Business Expert Press Human Resource Management and Organizational Behavior Collection

Collection ISSN: 1946-5637 (print)
Collection ISSN: 1946-5645 (electronic)

Cover and interior design by S4Carlisle Publishing Services Private Ltd., Chennai, India

First edition: 2019

10 9 8 7 6 5 4 3 2 1

Printed in the United States of America.

Special thanks to
Simon A. Collier for his support.
Writer, reader, friend.

Abstract

Business and fighting are two sides of the same coin.

Every businessperson engages everyday in small acts of negotiation and conflict; understanding what characterizes our conduct, and what are its strengths and weakness, will help us develop more effective relationships.

Chief Kickboxing Officer shows how the fighting and business mindsets cross over in this process of discovery and, in particular, what lessons can be learned from a highly refined and scientific type of fighting system: the martial arts.

By looking at four types of behavioral and leadership styles and mapping each of them onto a martial art, this book allows the readers to learn lessons best suited to their personality.

- Formal and proactive types that align with the martial art of karate.
- Formal and responsive types that align with the martial art of judo.
- Informal and proactive types that align with the martial art of Mixed Martial Arts (MMA).
- Informal and responsive types that align with the martial art of Brazilian Jiu Jitsu (BJJ).

"*Chief Kickboxing Officer* is not a book about fighting your way to the top of the corporate ladder. It's about applying the visceral, tactical lessons of martial artistry to the way we think and the way we interact with people" (Jonathan Clements).

Keywords

leadership; strategy; entrepreneurial; management; Asia; Japan; China; performance; communication

Contents

Foreword

By Jonathan Clements

I found myself on a plane to Japan once, sitting next to a man who was something big in the martial arts. He explained that he used to be a night-club bouncer, and that he wanted to stop fights without getting hurt. It was only after his martial arts training began that he applied what he was learning there to situations in his workplace. He could see a fight brewing and take away the fuel that could make it start in the first place. He learned how to pick troublemakers from the crowd, before they even entered the club, and he started to experiment with ways of talking them away from violent intent. After a few years, he left his old job and became a police negotiator. He's now the guy on speed dial when there's a weeping girl standing on the edge of a building or an angry young man with a knife to a shopkeeper's throat. There is more, he assured me, to martial arts—we created them to stop trouble, not start it.

Alfonso Asensio alludes in his opening pages to that motto of muscular 1980s capitalism: "business is war." But much of what he examines in the book you are about to read is based on a discovery from centuries earlier, that war was a business, and not always a profitable one.

Sun Tzu's *Art of War* was written, at least in part, to inform people about what a terrible investment violence could be. It was set up as a box-ticking exercise in tallying strengths, opportunities, weaknesses, and threats, like some ancient strategy app for armchair generals. Are you sure you have the upper hand? Do you have enough soldiers? Is there no way you can attain your goals without risk? The entirety of Sun Tzu's second chapter, "Going to War," details the hidden costs of any kind of fighting—widespread inflation, political anxieties, and mounting unrest.

I have no qualms about calling Sun Tzu a pacifist. Despite his sound-bite presence in practically every book about combat, his famous little book devotes much of its page-count to avoiding a fight at all costs. It's true that Sun Tzu does talk through some of the tactics of winning a battle, but he does so with a weary sigh, after he has repeatedly told the reader that fighting is a fool's errand, a waste of manpower and resources. Newcomers to the martial arts are often surprised at the degree to which this attitude crosses over in the practice hall—walking away from a fight, de-escalating angry situations, displaying a different kind of heroism.

Chief Kickboxing Officer is not a book about fighting your way to the top of the corporate ladder. It's about applying the visceral, tactical lessons of martial artistry to the way we think and the way we interact with people. As such, it also functions as a window to the diversity of ideas to be found in martial arts themselves—the thoughtful Jigoro Kano, struggling to get judo off the mat; the boisterous Gichi Funakoshi, fighting karate's corner, or the iconic Bruce Lee, ducking and diving through the creation of his mixed martial art. It also offers glimpses of some of the cultural interplay of martial arts, as found in popular fiction like the Musashi books or the *Romance of the Three Kingdoms*. I knew a lot of these stories before, but I was unaware of many of their echoes in corporate culture. Asensio's book, rich in anecdotal detail, prompts me to consider the image of Sun Tzu, sitting on a cloud somewhere, politely nodding while a ghostly Steve Jobs tries to demonstrate a Reality Distortion Field.

"Think different," as he might have said.

Jonathan Clements's publications include *A Brief History of the Martial Arts and The Art of War: A New Translation*.

Introduction

Business and Fighting

Business and fighting are two sides of the same coin.

This idea is hardly a novel notion; from the "business is war" motto that the aggressive corporate elite promoted in the 1980s to the multiple applications of *Art of War*, Sun Tzu's classic fifth-century BC Chinese text, in the business sphere, the relationship between both worlds has been explored at length.

The simple reason for that similarity is that both business (understood as a commercial activity as much as a negotiation aimed at reaching an agreement) and fighting happen when two parties desire to exploit the same scarce resource; such competitiveness breeds conflict, which, in turn, needs to be resolved. Historically, during mankind's most warring periods (and even nowadays), factions have fought for wealth, expansion, or predominance; similarly, in the modern economic era, companies and corporations contend for the consumer's attention and share of wallet. The basic dynamics of conflict barely change from one to another; only the way they are applied varies.

In the fertile valley of the Tigris and Euphrates rivers, where the first civilizations sprung up around the year 4,000 BC, settled human communities discovered this reality early on and engaged in a struggle to secure their survival, creating an ongoing status quo of competition. Often rivalries would be resolved via warfare, but, when possible, collaboration was the preferred solution and the deciding factor in this choice was cost: Which strategy was less taxing of resources? Was it better to negotiate and reach an agreement for a share of the total prize or engage the opponent militarily, suffering material and human losses in the process, in order to take it all?

On occasion, the line between fighting and business negotiation would be blurred. The Assyrian empire (2500 BC–605 BC) practiced an infamous scorched-earth policy when dealing with its adversaries, which (just as it happens with highly litigious companies nowadays) had less to do with human malice and more with a corporate-like strategy aimed at discouraging competitors and preventing similar conflicts in the future. Albeit with far more damaging cost in personal suffering, arson and pillaging were tools of negotiation for the ancient kings, just as the clauses of a contract are for modern enterprises.

But it is not only competitiveness that breeds conflict; personal interaction also creates friction between individuals. The collaboration required by human beings to found cities, expand empires, and build monuments in the ancient world was based on people working side by side and carried the same degree of stress and strains at the personal level that we see in offices and factories across the world today. The gripes and petty complaints about comrades and officers of a roman legionnaire walking Via Appia were probably not dissimilar to the ones a Taiwanese Marine or a City Hall accountant would voice nowadays.

This type of conflict also had to be resolved. First, because it was a violent age, by using violent means; but, as societies evolved, more and more conciliatory channels needed to be developed.

If human beings carry the capability to solve problems in both manners—via practical, amicable means as much as violent, forceful ones—should there not be, then, lessons that are common to both worlds, that is, business and fighting? The aim of this book is to add to our existing understanding by introducing fresh examples and ideas of how fighting and business mindsets cross over and, particularly, to offer a new perspective into what creates effective actions and interactions in the corporate world based on the learning of a particular, highly refined type of fighting system: the martial arts.

Why the Martial Arts?

Although initially intermingled, societies, over time, formalized these abilities for business and fighting into established, distinct professions. Those skilled in negotiating, gaining advantage, and settling disputes in a noncombative manner moved into the business and diplomatic worlds. Those who sought to achieve the same results via the use of force entered the field of qualified soldiering.

But human nature is not so easily channeled, and neither are work and tasks so easily compartmentalized. Every individual has a complex, ambiguous nature, and every single person, regardless of one's job role, engages daily in small acts of negotiation and conflict. As the writer Robert Heinlein put it:

A human being should be able to change a diaper, plan an invasion, butcher a hog, conn a ship, design a building, write a sonnet, balance accounts, build a wall, set a bone, comfort the dying, take orders, give orders, cooperate, act alone, solve equations, analyze a new problem, pitch manure, program a computer, cook a tasty meal, fight efficiently, die gallantly. Specialization is for insects.[1]

In other words, all humans are in part warriors; or at least should be. But once professional fighting became the restricted field of a small dedicated army, civilians were reduced to finding other, less lethal venues to practice combat and so were born the nonmilitary martial arts.

The term "martial arts" carry a strong cultural baggage, and, although Europe has a long tradition of civilian fighting, from the ancient and brutal Greek *pankration* or renaissance quarterstaff dueling to the ubiquitous sport of boxing, the very name "martial arts" is normally identified as an Asian cultural expression. This may be due to the fact that although Italy, France, or England developed solid civilian martial traditions, for the most part, they let them fade away in the wake of the technological developments, which rendered the systems obsolete. China, Thailand, the Philippines, and Japan, on the other hand, managed to maintain the martial tradition unvarying and isolated from technological military advancements. It is not for this book to say which knowledge adjusted better to the flow of history but Southeast and East Asian martial arts seem to have latched onto the idea that their systems went beyond fighting efficiency and offered a necessary outlet for a human compulsion regardless of their practicality.

Because of what martial arts tell us about the embedding of a combative activity in civilian society and the harnessing of instrumental

---

[1]R.A. Heinlein. 1973. *Time Enough for Love.* New York: Ace books.

aggression, this book will, in order to explore the connections between businesses and fighting mentality, use as reference four different types of fighting systems:

- Two are styles of Japanese origin (one Chinese inspired and another autochthonous to the archipelago) and are included because of their cultural impact and popularity.
- One has an East Asian origin but has been pushed through a Western filter to a degree that has created a completely original composite.
- One is a modern amalgam of different styles, and its relevance has as much to do with its fighting efficiency as with its self-promotional and business acumen.

CHAPTER 1

The Four Behavioral Styles

Behavioral Styles in the Business World

People are different, and those differences, while greatly enriching the never-ending process of personal interaction, also create friction.

Our capabilities and, particularly, how we apply them to deal with different tasks vary greatly from person to person and so do the expectations we have about how others deal (or fail to deal) with such tasks. This is apparent just by looking at daily work routine as it happens in the corporate environment; someone may be at the office and feel frustrated that the person at the other side of the table is just not understanding why a particular thing (a project, a process, a calculation) has to be done in a particular way. Managers may not understand why team members cannot complete an assigned task in the way they need them to, even when the reasons for it have already been explained. Or certain team members may be left scratching their heads and feeling frustrated, not understanding the instructions, so clear to some and confusing to others, that managers are delivering. Outside of work, day-to-day life is a parade of efforts in dealing with behavior types that are different to oneself. How often we get enraged because the person who is lining up in front of us is having trouble operating an ATM or is holding up the queue in the airplane aisle by trying to fit his or her luggage in a way that is obviously nonsensical . . . to us.

The truth of the matter is that, by living in society, people are destined to come across others who do not conform to the way they see things and the way they do things. And in a professional context, where performance is measured by communicational, relationship, and leadership abilities, the key to success may just be how to best broaden our own understanding of others rather than trying to change their behavior so it fits our expectations.

In fact, this is such an essential skill that it comes up immediately upon joining the professional world. In a job, any job, the initial step is always to be thrown in the midst of a group of strangers; we are not consulted about who we prefer to work with but are paired with coworkers based on skill or role, not personal compatibility. How we behave under such conditions reflects our temperament and affects, in turn, the attitude of those around toward us. Different types of people meshed together can work in harmony and turn out to have complementary behaviors, while others can become antagonistic and affect performance.

Even if we have no intention of changing the way we act, understanding what are the characteristics of our conduct, and what are its strengths and weakness, will help us develop more effective relationships (and it should be noted that "effectiveness" here is not used only in its purely utilitarian or mercantile sense; getting to know and establishing a meaningful personal friendship with a new acquaintance is as much a valid result of an effective relationship as closing a multimillion-dollar sales deal). In turn, knowing which type of behavior we can expect from those around us will remove unpredictability from our social interactions, increasing their positive effects and helping us lessen negative ones.

Such understanding is, in short, a key professional competence that allows us to work, communicate, and lead people of different characters who exhibit different behaviors, and it comes via two fundamental points of awareness:

- We need to recognize what our behavioral style is.
- We need to learn how to recognize the behavioral style of others.

The Legacy of Behavior Classification

The behavioral classification used in this book is based on the model developed by American psychologist William Moulton Marston (1893–1947). In a book published in 1928, *Emotions of Normal People*, Marston, a fascinating scholar who also developed the polygraph lie detector machine and created the comic book character "Wonder Woman," explained how people's emotions and behavior can be classified into four types depending on their predominant trait:

- Dominance (D), when there is a superiority of self over some sort of antagonist.
- Inducement (I), when there is a process of persuading someone, in a friendly way, to perform an act suggested by the subject.
- Submission (S), when there is a voluntary obedience to the commands of the person in authority.
- Compliance (C), when the subject is moving himself or herself at the dictates of a superior force.

This model had come to be known as the DISC classification and still influences research on human psychology to this day.

The book's curious title uses the word "normal" because Marston made clear that his intention was to classify people's standard behavior, that is, the type of actions they expressed when not under stress:

> I do not regard you as a "normal person", emotionally, when you are suffering from fear, rage, pain, shock, desire to deceive, or any other emotional state whatsoever containing turmoil and conflict. Your emotional responses are "normal" when they produce pleasantness and harmony. And this book is devoted to description of normal emotions which are so commonplace and fundamental in the every-day lives of all of us that they have escaped, hitherto, the attention of the academician and the psychologist.[1]

Despite the inherent complexity of the human psyche, Marston was not the first who looked into classifying people's behaviors into a model or chart that could be simultaneously simple and comprehensive. The Greek physician Hippocrates (c. 460–c. 370 BC) developed the idea that there exist four temperaments, each related to a natural element,

---

[1]W.M. Marston. 1928. *Emotions of Normal People*. London: Kegan Paul Trench.

in the rational mind, and that establish many types of archetypical personalities:

- Sanguine (air-like): Active, outgoing, and charismatic.
- Choleric (fire-like): Decisive and goal oriented.
- Melancholic (earth-like): Thoughtful, self-reliant, and analytical.
- Phlegmatic (water-like): Sympathetic, relaxed, and easygoing.

Hippocrates noted that those positive traits could be taken to their extreme and develop into negative behavioral patterns, which accounted for social and interpersonal frictions. The sanguine become risk-taking, the choleric become dictatorial, the melancholic become reclusive, and the phlegmatic become pusillanimous. As per the classical conception of physiology, displaying one or another behavior was ultimately attributed to varied humors of fluids present in the human body, which, in different combinations, determined a personality type. Hippocrates understood, however, that the human character is not always so easily explained and that there existed mixtures between the different types so that individuals could present at the same time characteristics of two or more of them.

The Swiss psychiatrist and psychoanalyst Carl Jung (1875–1961) also looked at the different personality trends present in each human being and how they "determine and limit a person's judgment." In his 1921 book *Psychological Types*, he identified two attitudes for the control of consciousness, introversion and extraversion, and four basic psychological functions:

- Thinking, the intellectual comprehension of things.
- Feeling, the judgment of the value of things based in a sentimental function.
- Sensing, the sensorial perception of the world.
- Intuiting, the adding of meaning through a deeper perception process.

Later, Katharine Cook Briggs and her daughter Isabel Briggs Myers developed the "Myers–Briggs Type Indicator," based on Jung's approach. Still widely used today, the indicator takes the form of a personal questionnaire where, by answering different questions, the participant profile is aligned with one of 16 different personality types that organize

Jung's principles into a list ranging from the ISTJ (Introversion + sensing + thinking + judging) group to the ENTP (Extraversion + intuition + thinking + perceiving).

When looking at the lessons that result from applying martial arts fighting mentality to business and business-related interactions, this book divides individual behavioral patterns into one of the four following groups, derived from Marston's original classification. Each name looks to represent a behavioral type that can be intuitively recognized in a professional environment:

1. The Controller
2. The Analyst
3. The Promoter
4. The Supporter

These four basic behavioral patterns are initially defined according to where they sit in a graph that defines human behavior as points articulated along two basic parameters or axes:

1. Formal/informal behaviors: Refers to the degree to which a person is task-oriented and likes to work under clearly stated rules, or is people-oriented and prefers a more fluid, unstructured environment.
2. Proactive/responsive behaviors: Refers to the degree to which a person uses a direct, take-charge type of approach or an indirect, more supporting one.

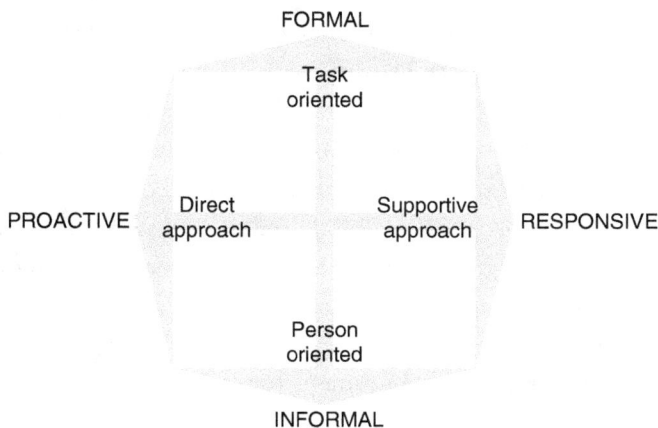

FORMAL

Task
oriented

PROACTIVE   Direct   Supportive   RESPONSIVE
             approach   approach

Person
oriented

INFORMAL

Understanding these two axes is the first step in learning what the individual behavioral patterns are.

The Vertical Axis: Formal/Informal Behaviors

In 2017, a conference took place in San Francisco hosted by the technology and media company Facebook. Following the informal and loose Silicon Valley style, the organizers chose an unusual venue, the Palace of Fine Arts, where a large warehouse had been conditioned with sofas, Wi-Fi service, chairs, barista coffee counters, and meeting rooms. There were two stages, one at each end of the large location; the first one, wider, was dedicated to business and sales presentations, while the second stage, narrower, was there for the engineering and technical discussions.

Over the course of 2 days, a pattern showing differences not just between the programs in both areas but about their style quickly emerged. The speakers on the sales stage were smartly dressed, used slides with a simple, evocative sentence, and pitched their ideas in an emotional, passionate manner. They talked about "partnership collaboration" and "synergy" and "market impact." The speakers on the technical stage were mostly engineers, dressed in comfortable, casual outfits; their slides had an abundance of detail, and although many of them seemed not very used to public speaking, their presentations were structured and logical.

It would be simplistic to say that each type of presentation style that day was exclusive to a certain work role; not all businesspeople were fast-talking salespersons, nor were all engineers social recluses who spoke in incomprehensible technical lingo. But it is true that an alignment of behavior with job roles could be felt: the business area was informal and people-oriented; the engineering one was formal and task-oriented. It certainly stands to reason: salesmanship requires a degree of gregariousness because results will be determined by the ability a person has to engage with clients and prospects. Similarly, technical jobs need, by definition, accuracy and attention to detail if a new program or machine is to work properly and without hitches.

In the classification of behavioral styles, these two broad types correspond to the gradating axis line, which goes from formal to informal:

1. The formal behavior style is task-focused and refers to people who follow a disciplined and structured working style. They are precise in their communication and present ideas in a less emotional way, staying close to facts and figures to support their arguments. In some cases, such formality can come across as obdurate.

2. The informal behavior style is relationship-oriented and refers to people who follow a less organized but more intuitive working style. Their communication style is less organized but more approachable, showing emotion that appeals to the listener's gut feeling rather than the intellect. In some cases, this informality can come across as fickle.

The Horizontal Axis: Proactive/Responsive Behaviors

In the 1938 comedy *Bringing up Baby*, Cary Grant plays David Huxley, a mild-mannered paleontologist who gets entangled with the young heiress Susan Vance, played by Katherine Hepburn. Grant's quiet academic life is upset when he is taken away by the energetic Hepburn in a series of antics and adventures, which include jail, a leopard, and a collapsing dinosaur skeleton.

The 1978 musical romantic comedy *Grease* saw these roles reversed when rocker Danny Zuko (John Travolta) falls for prim and proper Sandy Olsson (Olivia Newton-John) and manages to win her heart with a mixture of roguish charm, 1950s car races, and Travolta's trademark dance moves.

Nowhere is the at-times-opposing, at-times-complementary dynamic between active and passive temperaments more apparent than in romantic comedies, where writers and directors love to pair couples of opposite personalities and play them against each other for jocular effect. In the case of *Bringing up Baby*, Hepburn's vitality ends up impressing on Grant a joy of life he didn't know he had been missing. In *Grease*, Travolta's bad-boy persona reveals a wilder side in Newton-John, a transformation she exteriorizes at the end of the film.

Both pairs of characters are a simplified and extreme depiction of the proactive and responsive behaviors. Travolta and Hepburn are impulsive and energetic—they are the ones who move the plot ahead—while Grant and Newton-John are conservative and easygoing, and it is their transformation that gives a satisfying end to both movies. While in cinema the positive attributes of the proactive style in this dualism are highlighted to add drama, there is no inherent advantage to having one or another behavior. Both present merits and demerits and are balanced out by other traits that come together to define the full individual.

In the classification of behavioral styles, these two broad personality types correspond to the gradating axis line, which goes from proactive to responsive.

1. The proactive behavior style is, by definition, a more forceful one; it processes information in a direct manner and states that information with certainty. It is prone to challenging the status quo when taking action, and this often enables a more directional business style and out-of-the-box thinking. In some cases, such proactivity can come across as domineering.

2. The responsive behavior style is less vehement. Instead of issuing statements, it asks questions, which may be designed to lead to assumed answers. This is a thoughtful, indirect behavior, which can seem indecisive and works better when, as the name indicates, it reacts to an external stimulus. In some cases, this responsiveness comes across as indecision.

The Four Behavioral Styles: Natural Behavior and Adapted Behavior

Based on where along these two axes a person's conduct falls, four basic types of behavioral styles emerge:

1. Formal and proactive types result in *controlling* behavioral styles.
2. Formal and responsive types result in *analytical* behavioral styles.
3. Informal and proactive types result in *promoting* behavioral styles.
4. Informal and responsive types result in *supportive* behavioral styles.

FORMAL

Controlling ♜	Analytical ♞

PROACTIVE   RESPONSIVE

Promoting ♟	Supporting ♜

INFORMAL

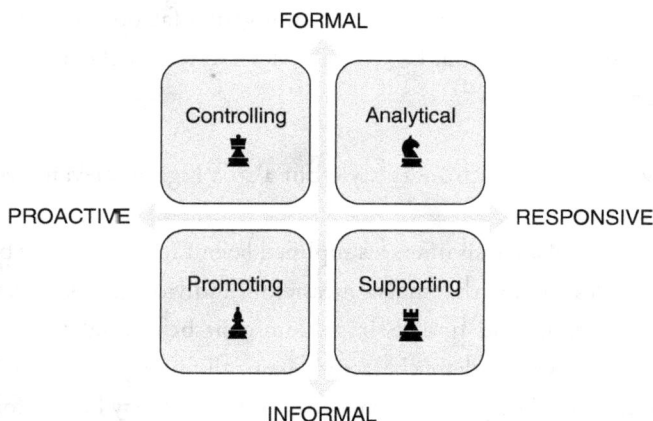

Although simple looking, this chart is a powerful tool for categorization. Once people identify and understand the behavioral style to which they belong, the chances of meeting somebody with the same characteristics are much smaller than meeting someone who doesn't share them. Roughly only one in every four other people[2] will have a similar understanding of how things should be done, while everybody else will hold a different set of priorities and a different understanding of what is important.

How do we align our wants and needs with such a large number of the population? How do we manage to work together to achieve a common goal when every aspect in this sentence (work, achievement, and goal) can have and often does have different connotations for everyone?

The key, again, is to understand others as much as to understand oneself.

Of course, personality and behavioral styles are just indicators of more complex individual traits, and being assigned to one or another is not an ancient Egyptian curse from where there is no escape; the objective is simply to learn how to be more effective in communicating and connecting with other styles as well as to accept our own personal limitations.

---

[2]Population split is not equal between the four types and varies according to some considerations, including the strength of the primary and secondary behavioral style. Here, 25 percent is assigned to each type for simplicity's shake.

Furthermore, there are two important mitigating factors when identifying assignments to the four behavioral styles that reduce the determinism of the chart:

1. Everybody has a primary style but also a highly relevant secondary one.
   Traditional analysis offers a simplified layout for personality behavior styles because that makes it easier for individuals to self-examine their actions and find their predominant behavioral traits. Most people, however, share characteristics of all four styles to one degree or another. As a primary analyst, an individual may be comfortable analyzing data in order to reach a decision, but how the person takes action on that decision and how he or she communicates it can vary a lot. An analyst with a secondary controlling type will act quickly, while an analyst with a secondary promoting style will choose a different path and develop a more creative solution. While both fall within the analytical range, their behavior will be notably different.

   Environment also plays a part. Although primary styles are quite stable through all contexts, different secondary styles come to the fore depending on particular situations. A relaxed home environment may enforce a supporting behavior, while a more challenging business setting calls for a controlling style.

2. Everybody can learn how to develop other personality traits.
   Human adaptability has a remarkable ability to deal with changes, and this extends to behavioral styles. A style can be modified or trained, either consciously or unconsciously, to expand its range and go well beyond its theoretical limitation, effectively moving along the formal/informal and proactive/responsive axes. If analysts find themselves in a position of leadership, they may develop a way to interact with their team so that they promote communication and team spirit, as a supporter or a promoter would do. Similarly, Supporters who have to tackle data-driven tasks can develop the analytical attention to detail that will allow them to work in that role.

The Four Business Behaviors and the Four Fighting Styles

Since the four behavioral styles, controller, analyst, promoter, and supporter, are defined according to their alignment with the two axes, formal/informal and proactive/responsive, it is necessary to classify the corresponding martial arts along the same lines.

Formal/Informal Axis

In the next chapters and when applied to martial arts, the formal/informal axis will have the following reading:

1. Formal fighting styles refer to those that follow a highly structured catalog of movement and apply them within the confines of drill practice or free sparring. Formal styles leave narrow room for personal adaptation of the techniques and require the practitioner to re-create the blueprint moves as closely as possible. Furthermore, these styles have a test-based process in place that regulates the progression through the ranks.

   The two formal styles selected in this book are karate and judo because of the following reasons:
   - They both have a clearly defined syllabus of techniques for each belt rank and a formalized exam that tests proficiency in that set of movements before moving on to the following rank.
   - They both use as a learning tool a set of movements or practice forms called *kata* which the practitioners employ to refine their ability.
   - They both require that all moves learned through practice are applied to free sparring with strict adherence to the standard.

2. Informal styles refer to those that use a loose set of movements built around a set of basic techniques; such moves are prone to be adapted by the practitioners based on personal style. Because of this, the progression through the ranks is not determined by the perfect re-creation of the standard but, rather, through the overall ability of the practitioners to seamlessly integrate the moves into free sparring.

The two informal styles selected in this book are Mixed Martial Arts (MMA) and Brazilian Jiu Jitsu (BJJ) for the following reasons:

- They place reduced emphasis on replicating a standardized syllabus of movements. The progression of the practitioner is based on performance rather than knowledge. Basic techniques are doctrinal nodes around which personal style is developed.
- They both dispense with the use of practice forms (*kata*).
- They place great emphasis on sparring practice because the objective is to demonstrate effectiveness when applying techniques against a live, resisting opponent.

Proactive/Responsive Axis

The proactive/responsive axis will have the following reading:

1. Proactive fighting styles will be those that initiate the action. This is particularly relevant with striking combat forms—those where hands, feet, elbows, and knees are used for attack, starting in an upright position. Even though these styles have a wide range of techniques that are used in response to an opponent attack (called counters), those too require a change of initiative and for the fighter to take the offensive.

   The two proactive styles selected are karate and MMA because of the following characteristic:

   - Their techniques require the application of explosive energy, both for attack and defense and for the submission of the opponent by inflicting impact trauma. Energy is generated not by balance or leverage but by using both body mass and weight distribution.

2. Responsive styles will be those that rely heavily on the opponent's action to apply their techniques. These are usually grappling fighting styles, where submission happens by unbalancing and throwing the opponent or by driving him or her into a position where he or she can be controlled.

   The two responsive styles selected are judo and BJJ because of the following characteristic:

   - They don't rely on the use of movement to generate explosive power but rather on balance changes and leverage, as well as redirecting the force of the opponent.

The correspondence between the four behavioral styles and the selected four martial arts is, therefore, as follows:

1. Formal and proactive types result in *controlling* behavioral styles, which align with the martial art of karate.
2. Formal and responsive types result in *analytical* behavioral styles, which align with the martial art of judo.
3. Informal and proactive types result in *promoting* behavioral styles, which align with the martial art of MMA.
4. Informal and responsive types result in *supportive* behavioral styles, which align with the martial art of BJJ.

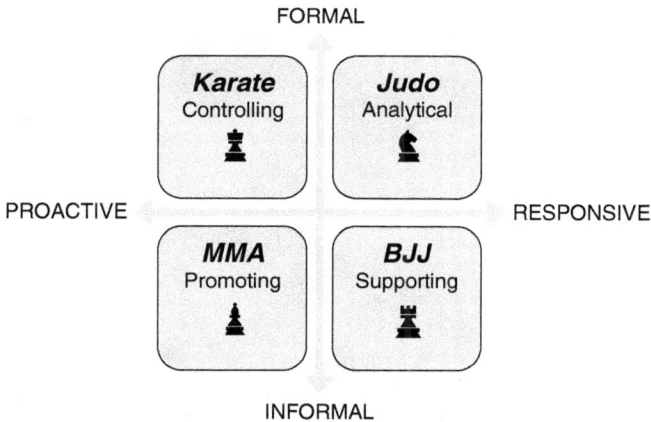

FORMAL

Karate Controlling	**Judo** Analytical

PROACTIVE   RESPONSIVE

MMA Promoting	**BJJ** Supporting

INFORMAL

CHAPTER 2

The Controller Style

CEO Use Case: Bill Gates, the Man Who Would Be King

Paul Allen, the business entrepreneur who cofounded Microsoft with Bill Gates in 1975, published years later a biographical book called *Idea Man*, which collected his experience in creating and launching the technology giant. Much of the attention the book generated was due to the chapters where Allen wrote about his working and personal relationship with Gates, a highly divisive figure both in his business and in his philanthropic ventures for the last 30 years.

In one particular chapter, Allen includes several anecdotes about Gates's managerial style, saying:

> Microsoft was a high-stress environment because Bill drove others as hard as he drove himself. He was growing into the taskmaster who would prowl the parking lot on weekends to see who'd made it in. People were already busting their tails, and it got under their skin when Bill hectored them into doing more. Bob Greenberg, a Harvard classmate of Bill's whom we'd hired, once put in 81 hours in four days, Monday through Thursday, to finish part of the

Texas Instruments BASIC. When Bill touched base toward the end of Bob's marathon, he asked him, "What are you working on tomorrow?"

Bob said, "I was planning to take the day off."

And Bill said, "Why would you want to do that?" He genuinely couldn't understand it; he never seemed to need to recharge.[1]

An article in the *Harvard Business Review* seems to echo and expand on this idea of Gates as a domineering leader:

> Gates is the achievement-driven leader par excellence, in an organization that has cherry-picked highly talented and motivated people. His apparently harsh leadership style—baldly challenging employees to surpass their past performance—can be quite effective when employees are competent, motivated and need little direction—all characteristics of Microsoft's engineers.[2]

Few stories resonate more with the general public than the rags-to-riches tale of a talented man. The technology industry, in particular, starting back in the 1970s seems a hub for exceptional individuals who, by sensing an opportunity or developing a brand-new technology, managed to change the world.

Bill Gates hardly fits the "rags" part of the story (his father was a prominent attorney and he enjoyed a comfortable upbringing) but the scale of the "riches" he achieved makes him a textbook example of success through determination. When he went from being a Harvard dropout to gaining the title of wealthiest man in the world, he did so by applying a radical mind-shift to the computer industry and looking at software as a business in order to fulfill his vision of placing a PC in every home (and having them all running Microsoft software).

Gates demonstrated early on in his career a style of leadership that was both task-focused and result-oriented, the two key components of the controller behavioral style. And control was, in fact, at the core

---

[1] P. Allen. 2011. *Idea Man*. New York: Portfolio/Penguin.

[2] D. Goleman, R.E. Boyatzis, and A. McKee. 2001. *Primal Leadership*. Daniel Goleman.

of his concept of management. Coming from a technical background, Gates could keep a close eye on the product development being done at Microsoft, and that, paired with his personal drive, made him a demanding leader. His employees were required to report regularly to him in order to present their progress, and during those sessions, Gates would constantly interrupt and challenge their facts and conclusions.

This inclination to micromanage his organization abated with time. Gates had achieved leadership responsibility early on in his life, but personal maturity as well as decades at the helm of Microsoft and his charitable foundation eventually tempered him. His conduct evolved into a more communicative form where he increasingly delegated responsibility for decision making to his team.

The Bases of the Controller Behavioral Style

The controller is often depicted in fiction as a take-charge type of person, the one who jumps to the fore to assume control in moments of crisis. This is John Wayne in *The Searchers*, Darth Vader in *Star Wars*, and Aragorn in *Lord of the Rings*. Also common is the trope of disaster movies where a leader rises in a situation of crisis: a person who knows what to do and how to organize the party to secure survival, and in many cases, the drama of the story comes from the contrasting view of those who regard him as a savior and those who see him as a despotic tyrant. That is, certainly, the dichotomy that best summarizes the nature of the controller.

All those characteristics (competence, decisiveness, autocracy, etc.) do appear in the controller behavioral type, but reality is, of course, more complex than fiction. The controller is defined, first and foremost, by his or her formal behavior, which favors processes and tasks over people or relationships, and secondly, by a proactive, domineering style; controllers follow what they consider is the right course of action without much regard for how those actions are perceived by the rest of the community.

The controller is a natural leader and his or her greatest advantage is the ability to create binomial cause–effect relationships by leveraging natural virtues toward concrete goals. This makes the controller especially suited for the world of enterprise, where driving processes from beginning to end is the correct recipe for success.

The controller is, therefore:

- A task-accomplisher → who delivers bottom-line results.
- A self-motivated worker → who initiates actions.
- A fast decision maker → who follows through with the results of such decisions.
- A disciplined worker → who also expects and demands efforts from others.

Although the controlling leadership style may seem like a natural fit for a CEO, it can become limited and, if applied in excess, move into the realm of authoritarianism, which has many shortcomings of its own. An excessively controlling leader can be impatient, dictatorial, and overbearing, therefore hampering the effectiveness of the organization rather than enhancing it.

The Controller at the Table: Negotiation and Communication Style

When it comes to communicating their ideas, controllers take a very characteristic top-down approach; these are businesspeople who are less interested in establishing a dialog than they are in conveying a set of directives that need to be applied. This communication style has positive traits because it is clear, unambiguous, makes good use of available resources, and is result-oriented. Highly hierarchical environments or those under recurrent pressure are a good fit for the controller, but these same attributes, at their worst, can lead to people's feelings being disregarded in favor of results, alienating other members of the community.

The controller communication style can also lose valuable inputs from other team members because of its noninclusive decision-making process. Furthermore, controllers tend to establish unidirectional communication lines, expressing an opinion and considering that to be an actual dialog.

When communicating with a controller, there are guidelines that would help any of the other three behavioral styles to more effectively engage his or her attention:

- The conversation needs to be clear and precise, avoiding rambling or excessive explanations.
- Argumentation works better if focused on the task at hand, and there is no need to make an effort to build personal rapport.
- Any disagreements should be contained to a particular issue and supported by facts, avoiding any emotional component.

The Controller at the Helm: Leadership Style

As mentioned before, of all the four behavioral styles, controllers are the ones who seem to fit best in a position of leadership because they are both organized and commanding. And because of their competitiveness, they are keen to absorb new roles and responsibilities, so the pressures of a dominant position are easier to assimilate for a controller than they are for any other behavioral style.

Controllers are surprisingly democratic, not in the decision system, where they see hierarchy as a natural status, but rather in the way they set high expectations for themselves the same as for everybody else. This is a very egalitarian perspective, where, with them at the steering wheel, everybody is under pressure to quickly and accurately deliver results for a large reward.

"Urgency" and "drive" are two key words for controller leaders, and they will make sure these are pushed down the organization so everybody feels the need to step up their game.

When reporting to a controller supervisor, the best way to gain his or her approval is to proactively work on solving the task at hand, all the while remembering that the controller is not concerned with process but with results. When working together, any other type of behavioral style benefits from the drive and brisk pace that the controller provides.

The Controller: Relationships Chart

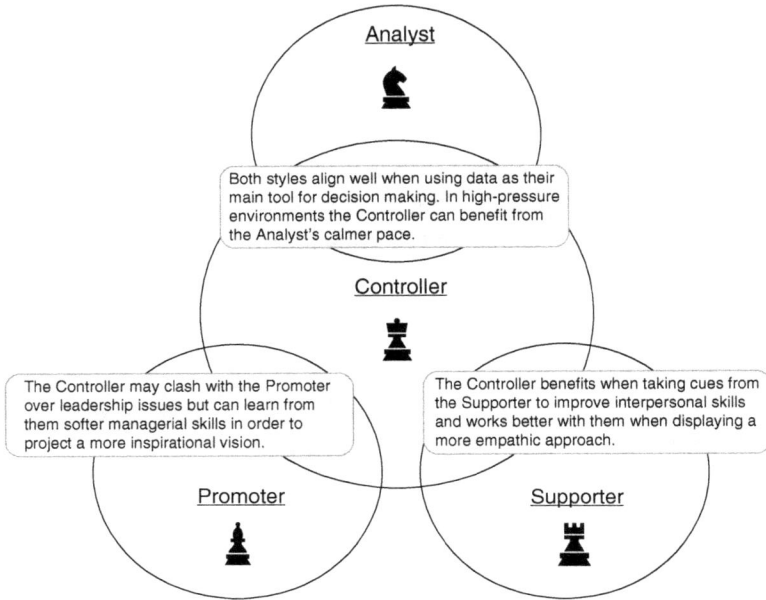

Analyst

Both styles align well when using data as their main tool for decision making. In high-pressure environments the Controller can benefit from the Analyst's calmer pace.

Controller

The Controller may clash with the Promoter over leadership issues but can learn from them softer managerial skills in order to project a more inspirational vision.

The Controller benefits when taking cues from the Supporter to improve interpersonal skills and works better with them when displaying a more empathic approach.

Promoter

Supporter

CHAPTER 3

Karate

The Controlling Fighting Style

The Making of Karate

In the mind of the general public, speaking about martial arts creates an image of ancient techniques secretively passed from generation to generation of masters, a relic of bygone eras that has miraculously survived until our modern age.

Although it is true that the common origins of most fighting systems can be traced eventually to previous, older forms of hand-to-hand combat systemization that is the same case with any other type of human enterprise, from dancing to pottery. In reality, the majority of the styles of martial arts as we know them nowadays have been codified in their current format fairly recently. The foundational dates for the three most popular Japanese styles, aikido, karate, and judo, can all be accurately pinpointed to the turn of the twentieth century, between the 1880s and the 1920s.

Although the origins of karate are very different from those of judo, there are striking similarities in the way they were introduced to the public at large and how they gained mass appeal. They both had an individual founder who acted as sort of catalyst, collecting a tradition of loosely related fighting styles and refurbishing them into a comprehensive, organized system with a strong educational and moral development component. In the case of karate, that person was Gichin Funakoshi, creator of the Shotokan school, which, although is only one of multiple styles of the art, is widely identified as synonymous with its practice.

Funakoshi was himself surprised by the changes he had brought and wrote in his memories:

> It was nearly four decades ago that I embarked upon what I now realize was a highly ambitious program: the introduction to the Japanese public at large of that complex Okinawan art, or sport, which is called karate-do "The Way of Karate." These forty years have been turbulent ones, and the path that I chose for myself turned out to be far from easy; now. Looking back, I am astonished that I attained in the endeavor even the quite modest success that has come my way.[1]

The success he achieved was far from modest, however. Same as his contemporary Jigoro Kano did with judo, Funakoshi managed to take an obscure martial art from the archipelago of Okinawa and transform it into a physical discipline followed by millions of students around the world.

Funakoshi was born in the Japanese coastal city of Naha, when it still maintained the name of Shuri, as it did when it was the capital of the old Okinawan kingdom of Ryukyu. Okinawa, or Ryukyu as it had been historically known, is a chain of islands that stretches all the way from the Japanese southwest across the Pacific until it almost reaches Taiwan. For centuries, the archipelago was under Chinese influence, as an independent kingdom first and as a vassal state later, and during this period, it is accepted by martial arts historians that continental styles of Chinese fighting forms made their way to the island and were adopted by the natives. By the seventeenth century, Okinawa had fallen under the Japanese sphere of influence, where it was to remain during the Meiji revolution and both World Wars until nowadays, and other styles, like the samurai wartime practice of jiu jitsu, made their way to the islands.

The dual impact that Chinese and Japanese martial arts had in the archipelago helps explain some of the peculiarities that developed in the Okinawan fighting tradition and modeled karate. A succession of repressive governments gave it an underground nature, which resulted in a secretive and austere style, very different from some of the flowery motions that are common to Chinese Wushu (or kung fu as it is widely known).

By the end of the nineteenth century, several masters were working in merging and systematizing the disparate Okinawan fighting styles, but Funakoshi was the one who was placed in the best position to promote the

---

[1]G. Funakoshi. 1975. *Karate Do: My way of life*. Kodansha US edition.

discipline, after moving from Naha to Tokyo in 1922. There, he started to apply a series of modifications, which helped the widespread acceptance of the system; first he changed the name his masters had used to refer to it. In Okinawa, each clan and family had had a different denomination for their particular, custom-made format of karate: Goju-ryu, Shorin-ryu, and so on depending on their distinct traits while the all-compassing word "kara-te" was translated as "China hand" ("China" referring to the historical origins of the practice and "hand" meant unarmed combat) and used as very generic term. By changing the Chinese-written ideogram "China" to "empty," the phonetic reading remained the same, "karate," but the meaning changed to "empty hand," which was both suitable to the new revamped style and more palatable for the increasingly nationalistic Japanese prewar government. Funakoshi also adopted the white practice uniform and colored belt system that judo's founder, Jigoro Kano, had made popular, and with that, the revived karate made its way into university practice halls and sport institutions before jumping to the international stage after the U.S. occupation of Japan of 1945.

Karate and the Search for Kinetic Excellence

As mentioned before, karate is hardly a unified discipline to this day. What we commonly refer to as karate is the Shotokan style, the one originally established by Funakoshi, but there exist dozens of other schools, some much older than Shotokan and some as recent as the very popular full contact Kyokushin-kai style, created in the 1960s.

But all in all, these styles share some common foundations: karate is a fighting style that uses the four limbs as weapons ("hands and feet are spears" read a foundational karate document) and training is aimed at developing power by optimizing the speed and force with which they are used. Kinetic energy is at the base of the practice of karate and it is used to attack, defend, and move.

Training is divided into three formats: drills, forms, and sparring:

1. Drills (*kihon*).

    These include the basic techniques of striking, blocking, and kicking and follow a highly structured program based in repetition. A number of assigned moves have to be practiced continuously and mastered before the practitioner can progress to the next level.

2. Forms (*kata*).
   These are a dynamic style of solo practice where basic techniques are chained together into a prearranged pattern.
3. Sparring (*kumite*).
   This is a free-form bout between two practitioners. Each school and federation follow different rules, but generally, the objective is to score points by hitting the opponent with hands and feet. Grabbing or wrestling is either not allowed or very limited.

Karate uses a wide variety of striking techniques, which are delivered in multiple ways (using palms, fingers, knuckles, elbows, knees, heels, etc.) and directions (forward, sideways, backward, upward, downward), emphasizing the idea that a karate practitioner must be able to hit from any position with virtually any part of the body. Many of these strikes are performed in a counterintuitive manner, whose effectiveness is a result of decades of experimentation, and need to be trained extensively before they can be applied.

For example, the most natural punching motion for human beings is the haymaker strike, an uncontrolled but powerful looping swing, which can be performed naturally without training due to its circular trajectory and generation of a large amount of power in relation with the mass of the arm. It is, however, easy to block and difficult to aim properly, so a more effective punching method is the karate straight blow. Learning to throw strikes in a straight line has two advantages:

- It delivers a much faster punch, the straight line being the shortest distance between two points.
- It allows the thrower of the blow to put the force of the hips and the whole body behind the attack instead of relying only on the strength of the arm.

Similarly, karate's chief characteristic is the use of kicks. Logic dictates that lifting one foot from the floor during a confrontation has the risk of limiting mobility as well as loosing balance, but with proper training, it gives the ability to multiply the body weapons used for offence from two to four as well as the possible angles of attack. Furthermore, being able to deliver a blow that uses the powerful leg muscles gives the karate practitioner a substantial advantage.

It can be said, therefore, that the practice of karate is the search for kinetic excellence; the ultimate objective of the art is the ability to move in the most effective way, a way that must be fast, powerful, and economic in its energy expenditure.

Karate's Business Learnings for the Controller

The formal aspects present in the controller mean this is a behavioral style that favors having complete control of his or her work and the circumstances that surround it. But business environments are, by their very nature, mutable; personal and social interactions converge with economic and technological processes, creating a complexity that can be unpredictable. This puts the controller under constant pressure; the fear of losing control can throw the controller into panic, to which he or she responds by resorting to the extreme aspects of his or her behavior and becoming dictatorial.

Karate, as well, suffers when under pressure. It is a very linear style, where attacks happen by making dashes into the opponent's defenses looking to strike. Although karate practitioners put a great deal of focus on blocks and parries to cover this eventuality, they, the same as the controller, are at their worst when the initiative is taken away.

Karate has developed a system that looks to prevent this by using forms or *kata*, sets of formalized technique-based movements that are conducted in a sequential motion. Although *kata* is practiced as a solo form, constant repetition familiarizes the practitioner with the flow of fighting and tries to provide an answer to the different situations he or she may face when sparring. For a controller struggling in a business environment, the concept of *kata* can be applied almost directly, because it concerns the creation of a repeating routine that deals with problem resolution by setting up a step-by-step process practiced until perfection. This is a solution that calls directly to both the formal and the proactive nature of the controller; crisis-solving rehearsal helps reduce the sense of unpredictability and helps maintain the habit of control.

But achieving proficiency in *kata* is not just a matter of repeating moves; to truly internalize its benefits, the karate practitioner needs to understand that there is a method in play. This method can be divided into three levels both in karate and in business:

1. The mechanical level.

   At this initial stage, the practitioner starts by blindly repeating a set of knowledge that is given to him or her by his or her instructor. For a karate student, it is an initial *kata* form; for an intern at a company, it is the mind-numbing task of arranging data spread sets, preparing presentations, and setting up meetings. But in both cases, the objective is the same: to prepare novices to accept the new environment by exposing them to specialized knowledge, to have them learn the rituals and protocols of interaction with other actors, to have them understand the existing hierarchy and their own position on it. At the mechanical level, performance has to be just like that, mechanical. There is no need to understand the why, just the how. Once novices prove they can perform, it is time to move to the next stage.

2. The understanding level.

   Once practitioners demonstrate they can function within the new environment and have learned the basic moves, they can start developing the work that is required from them and learning becomes a conscious act, not a mechanical one. At the understanding level, constant exposure to routine brings awareness of detail; the karate student finds not-so-obvious dimensions in the *kata* he or she has practiced a thousand times and starts applying that insight when learning more advanced moves, and the reasons a certain block, move, or spin is there become more obvious; thus, the student is able to perform the *kata* with higher degrees of precision. Similarly, interns discover the reason behind the specific formatting of documents and start applying that insight into new chores; they learn what the ebb and flow is in the relationships with other teams and companies and understand how to anticipate and respond to crisis and business changes. There is pause here to think, to analyze what is being done in order to do it well.

3. The internalization level.

   At this final stage, the actions of the practitioner go back to a certain automatism that is similar to the mechanical level but with a big difference: the rote-learning process is not there anymore; now intuition takes its place. The system—the fighting system, the business system—has been internalized to such a level that subtleness takes over and no pause for thinking is necessary. The fighter fights and drills with movements that have become second nature; the businessperson responds to the demands of daily activity with an effectiveness that is equally based on knowledge and experience.

The controller is a person of method, and the practice of *kata* is the essence of method. At its core lies the distillation of moves to a systematized format that prepares for the real fight. By applying the *kata* methodology to a business routine, the controller can prepare for the changes in his or her environment and bring a measure of certainty to an uncertain world.

CHAPTER 4

Learning from the Classics

A Book of Five Rings

A Vagabond's Legacy

In the morning of a spring day in 1612, two men met at a beach in the island of Ganryu off the coast of Japan.

One of them was a neat, well-dressed youth, a wealthy member of the samurai class that ruled the country for over 200 years. He was also one of the most famous sword-fighters in the country, already weapons master for the Hosokawa Lord despite his young age. The other man was much less impressive, a derelict-looking character with threadbare clothes and unkempt hair, someone more similar to a vagrant than a professional warrior.

The first man, named Sasaki Kojiro, was, according to legend, furious because his adversary had arrived over 3 hours late, something inadmissible by samurai etiquette and especially so because this was not a spur-of-the-moment duel. Both swordsmen had known each other by reputation for years and several notable lords, supporting one or the other, had intervened to arrange the encounter.

Kojiro started the fight angry, throwing (again according to legend) the scabbard of his sword away. His opponent, one Musashi of the village of Miyamoto, was holding a wooden makeshift weapon fashioned out of a spare oar he found while in route to the island.

The novelized version of the episode, published in the book *Musashi*, by the Japanese writer Eiji Yoshikawa in 1935, has Musashi reacting to Kojiro's anger by saying, "by throwing your scabbard away you proved you just lost." There is no record of what was really spoken by both swordsmen, but regardless of any banter they may have exchanged at the beach shortly after the duel started, Musashi had a cut in his tunic, while Kojiro lay dead from a strike to the head. The bout captured the imagination of seventeenth-century Japan, which was an isolated, feudal country at the time, and propelled Musashi to legendary status as the greatest swordsman who ever lived.

But perhaps the most interesting learning of the story is how Musashi fought as much with his mind as he did with his hands. He actually started the duel hours before both men met and was not late by caprice; his intention was to unnerve the veteran Kojiro. His weapon, as well, was something the other samurai was not prepared for. The wooden oar he crudely carved had a longer reach than the weapon of his opponent and was, in Musashi's hands, as lethal as any steel blade. Whatever comments he made during the fight were, no doubt, aimed to goad the other man to commit a mistake he could exploit.

We know for certain that strategy and correct mental attitude were a constant in the fighting philosophy that Musashi used to survive over 60 duels similar to the one in Ganryu because he told us. In the few years before his death by natural causes, Musashi retired to a cave to live ascetically while writing his posthumous work, a fencing and fighting treatise he would cryptically call *A Book of Five Rings*.

Violent Life in Violent Times

Today, the figure of Miyamoto Musashi and his book are well known in Japan, where he represents the epitome of the *bushido*, or code of conduct, of that famed national warrior class, the samurai.

Born Shinmen Musashi No Kami Fujiwara No Genshin in 1584 in Mimasaka province, Musashi (Miyamoto being the town where he lived as a child) was the son of minor gentility. He fought on the losing side of the battle of Sekigahara that initiated the *Bakufu* period, where the military governor of Japan, the Tokugawa Shogun, managed to finally close the period of civil strife that had engulfed the country and took steps to isolate the archipelago from foreign influences. This policy would remain in place until Japan opened again to the world during the Meiji restoration of 1868.

With no family fortune or powerful connections, Musashi became a wandering duelist and student of the martial arts, particularly Japanese fencing. During the period of peace, which followed the establishing of the shogunate, the role of the samurai warrior class shifted. There were no more wars to fight, so from being professional soldiers, they became more akin to civil servants or office workers involved in running the administration of the hierarchical and complex feudal state. Their martial ardor, also, needed to be transferred from the battlefield to the practice yard, and soon fighting schools sprung all over Japan, with dueling (both one-to-one and one-to-many) becoming the standard by which fighting skill was judged. While Musashi was part of the samurai class by birth, he didn't have a role in any of the local clans so, nearly destitute, he ended up a *ronin*.

This somewhat over-romanticized word was more prosaic than our modern understanding would have it. In seventeenth-century agricultural Japan, wealth was measured in rice and the only way for a samurai to keep a certain standard of living was by attaching himself to a lord and living off his state's income. A *ronin* had no access to this source of income and often resorted to robbery to survive. However, the lack of obligations of the *ronin* life paired well with the carefree nature of Musashi, and he spent years moving up and down the different islands, visiting fencing schools, and learning new fighting styles, concerned only with the way of the sword.

Musashi's travels and achievements are well documented. The Japan of his time was a highly literate society and his name comes up in almanacs, records, and diaries of the period. It is estimated that by the age of 29, he had won over 60 deadly duels, in occasion against more than one opponent. Then the fight with Kojiro took place and his fame rocked the country. As of that moment, Musashi stopped using steel swords in his duels. He was invincible.

Musashi retired from fighting in 1643 to open a school based on his own fencing style, a highly pragmatic system that differentiated itself by abandoning the traditional samurai two-hand grasp of the sword and using one blade in each hand. The master led a quiet life as an anchorite in a cave, where he spent his time meditating on the essence of fencing. During that time, he wrote *A Book of Five Rings*, dedicated to his pupil Teruo Nobuyuki, and completed it just a few weeks before his death on May 19, 1645.

The book is not purely about fencing (although it contains elements of sword fighting), but it is rather, and in Musashi's words, "a guide for those who want to learn strategy." It should be noted that by strategy, he means strategy in all fields, not just fighting; strategy in life, which gives it a much broader framework than the merely martial. It is, in summary, a catalog of behavior for how to overcome obstacles.

A Book of Five Rings

Although the myth surrounding Musashi makes it difficult to get an accurate picture of the man himself (Yoshikawa's book, an idealized account of his life, which has been turned into numerous films, did a lot to popularize the legend but little to represent the person), the interest of his work is indisputable. *A Book of Five Rings* is the writing of a man forged by the traditions of Taoism, Buddhism, and Confucianism that flooded into Japan from the third to the sixth century, and as such, it can be considered the distillation of numerous inherently Asian concepts as well as that of the samurai doctrine called *bushido* (the fact that *bushido* may be considered less of an aspirational warrior code and more of an institutional construct used to regulate the military class is part of a different conversation).

The lessons dictated by Musashi are simple and effective and, because of that, equally applicable to the world of negotiation as to the world of fencing. His constant preaching about the importance of having an attitude of improvement and a vision of victory not only on the battlefield but also in all aspects of everyday life aligned very well with the combative disposition of Japanese industry in the bubble years of the 1970s and 1980s, and *A Book of Five Rings*, the same as the *Art of War*" by Sun Tzu, was part of the battery of texts that Japanese businessmen used to study in order to put themselves at the forefront of global business.

The book, as its name implies, is divided into five sections:

1. The Book of Water.
2. The Book of Earth.
3. The Book of Fire.
4. The Book of Wind.
5. The Book of the Void.

Each one of the sections corresponds to an element that serves as a summary for the type of attitude that needs to be applied to overcome a certain set of obstacles.

1. The Book of Water—How to Retain Flexibility and Harness the Power of Abstraction

   With water as a base, the spirit becomes liquid. The water adopts the shape of its container, it is sometimes a stream and sometimes a sea. . . . If you master the principles of the sword, when you defeat a man, you defeat any man. The spirit necessary to defeat a man is the same spirit necessary to defeat ten million. The strategist turns small things into big things. The principle of the strategy is to know ten thousand things knowing one thing.

   In addition to the classical principle of water flexibility, which appears repeatedly in the Taoist tradition (and more recently in anything from Bruce Lee's quotes to automobile advertising), Musashi indicates that the procedures and mentality necessary to achieve success and overcome obstacles are the same at any scale, large or small. What is often missing is the training and discipline to recognize the patterns of similarity.

   Developing this mindset in a business and professional environment, an environment that is unstable by nature and where teams, jobs, projects, and scope change continuously, can provide a critical ability to quickly adapt to new situations. Informal styles like the supporter or the promoter may find adapting this principle easier than formal ones.

2. The Book of Earth—How to Maintain a Global Vision.

The body of the Path of strategy from the point of view of my school Ichi is explained in the Book of the Earth. It is difficult to understand the true Way only through fencing. Know the smallest things and the biggest things, the shallowest things and the deepest things. As if it were a straight road mapped out on the ground, this book is called the Earth Book.

Musashi was famous for including disparate elements in his fighting style, in contradiction to the seventeenth-century samurai tradition that advocated orthodoxy and respect for the form established by each particular school in fencing. Musashi found that such a restrictive approach as he saw in other fighters resulted in a very narrow outlook. Throughout his life, he was a keen student of all things and looked to continuously incorporate learnings from disparate fields of knowledge into his fencing.

The same can be said in terms of business ability: job specialization, where each person fulfills a specific role, is an unavoidable requirement of industrial society, and it helps increase effectiveness, but it should not run contrary to having a global vision. Developing a disposition that incorporates learnings from very different sources, even if they are removed from the specific field of work, is a key advantage. As Musashi surmised, there cannot be real understanding in any field of activity without some sort of understanding of the world as a whole. Informal styles, again, may find applying this principle easier than formal ones because of their inherent flexibility and inquisitiveness.

3. The Book of Fire—How to Remain Proactive in All Situations

This book is about combat since the spirit of fire is fierce, whether the fire is small or large; that is the way it is with combat. The Way of the battle is the same for the one-on-one fight as for battles with ten thousand warriors. You must appreciate that the spirit can become small or big. What is great is easy to perceive, what is small is difficult. The essence of this book is that you must train day and night to make quick decisions.

Musashi emphasized the need to be constantly proactive. Preparation is key because failure can come as easily in the small details as it does in the big decisions. He advocated regular training but expanded the importance to be constantly proactive to other areas that may influence the result of the battle, such as scanning the environment, actively forestalling the enemy, and, in general, tirelessly analyzing the fight from all possible angles until resolution.

This is a skill that very intuitively connects with the world of enterprise. The enemy of success is complacency on the one hand and poor preparation on the other. Proactive styles like the promoter or the controller will find applying this principle comes as second nature because of their constant drive to achieve results, while responsive styles will need to reinforce the need to step out of their comfort zone.

4. The Book of Wind—How to Accumulate and Retain Knowledge

This book is not concerned with my Ichi school but with other schools of strategy. By Wind I mean old traditions, present-day traditions, and family traditions of strategy. It is difficult to know yourself if you do not know others.

In his search for adaptability and efficiency, Musashi did not proclaim that only search and experimentation were the keys to success. He realized that before being able to do that, it was necessary to have a good knowledge of orthodox doctrine and established methods, which serves as a solid foundation. Only then is it possible to know where the limits are and how to expand them. He was also very aware of the newness of his own school of fighting and excluded it from this section.

Knowledge in this case is about ourselves, our allies, and our opponents, and in the business world, this means personal training and preparation, industry knowledge, market knowledge, and a keen understanding of competitors. The data-driven analyst behavioral style is the best match for adapting these learnings with the controller a close second; it is easy for both to accumulate information before making a decision. The promoter and the supporter, on the other hand, can find here reasons why their thought process needs to be filtered via data.

5. The Book of the Void—How to Relate to Nature and Accept What We Don't Know

> By emptiness I mean that what has no beginning or end. Reaching this principle means not reaching the principle since the path of strategy is the path of Nature. When you appreciate the power of Nature and understand the rhythm of each situation you will be able to reach your enemy naturally and hit him naturally. My intention is to teach how to follow the true Way according to Nature.

The last section is the most cryptic that Musashi wrote. In his conclusion, he seemed to having added a cautionary note about having an overeagerness for systematized planning and strategy, even though *A Book of Five Rings* is precisely that, a full text of tactical advice. In the end, there are no rules, since any path we follow sends us back to Nature and Nature is, ultimately, unknowable.

In the world of business, there also needs to be an understanding that some things are beyond control and there exists an inherent randomness in any human process. While the learning here should not be one of blind resignation, a well-rounded professional must know when to give up and move on.

The Way

There is a concept that makes a constant appearance in *A Book of Five Rings* and is more central than even that of strategy. For Musashi, the purpose of life was to find balance and his place in Nature through the constant search for the Way (known in Japan as *Do* and in China as *Tao*). He explained that the Way was a method of personal realization and understanding of the world but articulated through a specific activity. Such activity need not be restricted to the martial pursuits but could be anything from fencing and strategy to artistic processes or even the most mechanical and repetitive jobs.

In *A Book of Five Rings*, Musashi presented a series of basic rules that needed to be applied diligently in order to find the Way. This was not a task of a few days, a few months, or even a few years; it was a lifelong endeavor but it was also, for him, the only way a person could live fully.

- Do not think dishonestly.
- The Way is achieved by training.
- Familiarize yourself with all arts.
- Meet all professions.
- Develop intuitive judgment and understanding of everything.
- Perceive what cannot be seen.
- Pay attention even to the smallest things.
- Do not do anything that is not useful.

Reading this set of principles, one can find that there are evidently some common themes within each one of the sections in *A Book of Five Rings*: Prepare yourself by being both a specialist and a generalist to a point where knowledge is so ingrained in your actions that it appears intuitive.

Finally, after looking at both his work and his philosophy, Musashi's principles can be summarized in three rules for life that govern not only professional activities but also personal actions, three rules that any of the behavioral types can benefit from:

1. You must be effective.
2. You must be inquisitive.
3. You must be flexible.

CHAPTER 5

The Analyst Style

CEO Use Case: Elon Musk, A Data-Driven Leader

> When I was a little kid, I was really scared of the dark. But then I came to understand, dark just means the absence of photons in the visible wavelength—400 to 700 nanometers. Then I thought, well, it's really silly to be afraid of a lack of photons. Then I wasn't afraid of the dark anymore after that.

That quote comes from Elon Musk, CEO of Tesla and SpaceX, an entrepreneur, investor, and engineer famous for his relentless drive and attention to detail. It is also the kind of thing a person with a primarily analytical behavior would say when choosing how to look at the world: by reducing it to facts and evaluating the results in order to gain control over it.

For Musk, this is not an abstract principle; he applies this approach on a daily basis as leader of his different companies. The business magazine *Forbes* published an article in 2017 that showcased the impact of his distinctive managerial style even when applied to something as mundane as company meetings. Only in the United States, company employees sit through a staggering 11-billion meetings each year, and, as anybody who has ever worked in an office can testify, many of them are very unproductive.

But, as the writer puts it, "with his fiercely driven personal style, he [Musk] has elevated the practice of efficient meetings to a science."[1] In order to do this, he follows several principles:

- *He urges people to prepare properly to prevent poor performance.* Musk is a meticulous businessperson, and he requires from those attending or organizing meetings that they come prepared so no time is wasted with unnecessary explanations. Presenters should have all data at hand and are under pressure to explain and answer any follow up any questions that look to dig deeper into the subject; they are required to have a deep understanding of the whole subject and not only the slides being presented. Attendants should also study the issue before hand in order to ask only that which they may not understand.
- *He urges people to analyze granular facts.* . . Rather than discussing general issues or holding vague conversations, Musk demands from his teams that they continuously refer to basic facts so the meeting stays grounded and specific actions points and follow-ups can be decided. His attention to detail and tremendous memory make it difficult for his employees to get away with any inaccuracies.
- . . .*[B]ut keeping in mind strategic goals.* Musk is famous for his dogged perseverance when chasing up his goals. It is his opinion that daily work is littered with difficulties and failures, but keeping the big picture in mind and striving toward the final goal is what allows a company to progress. In meetings, the granularity of specific data has to be aligned with a strategic vision.

Data-driven, task-focused, being concerned about quality, and performance—all of these are characteristics of the analytical behavioral style, and, in Musk's case, they are reinforced by a strong promoting secondary type of behavior that allows him to drive and inspire his team.

---

[1]Forbes. 2017. "How Does Elon Musk Run His Famously Efficient Meetings?" *Forbes Magazine*, from the Isabelle Daigle original.

The Bases of the Analyst Behavioral Style

The analytical behavioral style is defined by its affinity with knowledge and data. This type of person communicates with the world by looking at all available information and leveraging it to make objective decisions.

Before taking any action, the analyst follows a specific process in which they:

1. Gather all the data.
2. Define and clarify parameters.
3. Produce a course of action based on the findings of 1 and 2.

The analyzer is that friend or relative who tends to plan trips in minute detail, the one who, when deciding to organize a party, starts planning the logistics and provisions, the number of attendants, the details of the venue. In fiction, the role of the analyst character is to expose information and to act as an agent of the audience, helping them to keep track of the story; it is the cautious planner, the strategist, and his role is to slow the pace of the plot, analyze the problem, and, often, come up with a solution, such as Mr. Spock in *Star Trek*, Lisa in *The Simpsons*, Hermione in *Harry Potter*.

In work settings, the analyst enjoys an organized approach and focuses on quality and accuracy, expertise and competency. Because of the analysts' formal leaning on the vertical axis, they prefer to focus on completing tasks, even individually, rather than interacting with people, although their efficiency and responsiveness means they can be good team players as well.

The analyst's behavioral style can be exasperating for other types, especially those of an informal nature like the promoter or supporter, who see the analyst as overly serious, inflexible, and overdetailed. And indeed, the biggest drawback of the analyst style is that, because he or she likes to have time to plan before acting, the person doesn't work well under pressure. When under constraint or in a tense environment, the analyst will often adopt a defensive position where he or she clamps down and becomes surly and unresponsive.

The analytical behavior works best when combined with a secondary controlling or promoting style, one where the person is more prone to take initiative, and it is in those cases, as seen in Elon Musk, when the data-driven nature of the analyst combines with a more proactive approach to produce a very effective leader.

The Analyst at the Table: Negotiation and Communication Style

During negotiation and while in conversation, the analyst is consistently a good listener. The analyst's interest in gathering data means he or she will be happy to talk to others, although their interpersonal skills may be stiffer than those of other informal styles. And, since the analyst is not keen on creating conflict, discussions and arguments will be civil and logical. When a solid, well-reasoned argument is presented, it will be accepted even if they do not agree with it.

The analyst has an ingrained aversion to risk that comes from the need to be as well organized as possible, so when something is not clear, when there is room for ambiguity, the person will feel uncomfortable. Effective conversations with the analyst, therefore, are those that convey information with precision and in detail.

When delivering information, on the other hand, the analyst will make sure they are providing all background facts; on occasion, this can be more than necessary, so it is critical that the analyst add a layer of actionable points to help others take action and gain specific results. During a negotiation process, appealing to their expertise for counsel will put analysts at ease and allow them to willingly share more information.

The Analyst at the Helm: Leadership Style

The source of authority for the analyst leader does not come from his or her communication skills or inspirational qualities. Rather, this is a leader who relies on well-established rules and proven standards in order to run the workflow efficiently. Analysts can assure their team that the organization that has been set up is optimal and that the decisions they make will be fair and objective.

Their biggest pitfall when interacting with a team, however, is an acute risk that the perspective analysts take may feel detached. For example, when they are conducting performance reviews, there is little question that these will be both fair and based in facts, not opinions. This can, however, appear as discouraging if it does not incorporate some flexibility based on other "intangible" variables, like personal issues or emotional circumstances.

People working for an analytical-type supervisor will need to be well prepared any time they interact with him or her, by having facts and figures at hand so they can back up any proposal, plan, or idea.

The Analyst: Relationships Chart

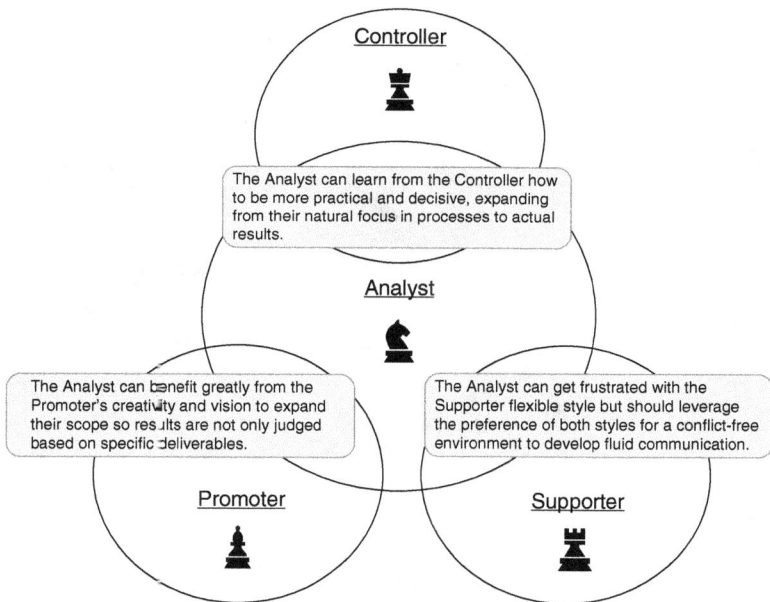

Controller

The Analyst can learn from the Controller how to be more practical and decisive, expanding from their natural focus in processes to actual results.

Analyst

The Analyst can benefit greatly from the Promoter's creativity and vision to expand their scope so results are not only judged based on specific deliverables.

The Analyst can get frustrated with the Supporter flexible style but should leverage the preference of both styles for a conflict-free environment to develop fluid communication.

Promoter

Supporter

CHAPTER 6

Judo

The Analytical Fighting Style

The Creation of Judo

Jigoro Kano's timing was perfect. At any other moment, his obscure training system, created in 1882 as a hybrid of different schools from an older, obsolete samurai method of unarmed combat, would have been, at best, a footnote in history. But at the turn of the twentieth century, Japan found itself at the crux of two radical transformations: One was an industrial modernization process, which would in time take the country from a feudal economy to a position that ranked it among the modern nations of the world and was crystalized with its victory over the mighty Russian empire in the war of 1905, an unthinkable feat for a nation that until a few decades before had been isolated from the world for over 200 years.

The second transformation was a progressive descent of the Japanese government and society into a repressive state, wielding a militaristic national policy, which saw the expansion of the Japanese empire through China, Korea, and Southeast Asia and culminated with its defeat by American forces at the end of World War II.

When Jigoro Kano (1860–1938) completed his systematization of judo, he encountered unprecedented government support to promote it because the new discipline tapped neatly into those two transformations. It was scientific in its study of human biomechanics and its pedagogic teaching method, and it had an unmistakable martial nature that recovered the Japanese warrior tradition and, removing its more lethal aspect, created a curriculum of bodily training that could help develop the next generation of Japanese soldiers.

Kano himself was physically less than impressive. He stood 158 cm and weighted 50 kg; a bookish, quiet young man who attended Tokyo Imperial University. After graduation, he became an educator, working first as a professor and then as a principal in different institutions. Encouraged by a family friend, he started training in the traditional and often-brutal unarmed fighting style of Jujutsu (also known as jujitsu or jiu-jitsu) to compensate for his lack of size and strength. But Japan's Edo period, what we think of as the era of the samurai, had just ended with the creation of the constitutional government of Meiji, and the warrior traditions were seen as retrograde and were quietly washed away, so Kano had trouble finding a suitable teacher. What is more, Jujutsu was far from being a centralized and organized system; each instructor he found specialized in one particular aspect of the art and the instructors often had glaring gaps in their repertoire of movements.

Kano's educational instinct took over, and, in a few years, the young master had integrated the disparate schools into a single, cohesive new method that moved away from the aggressive roots of Jujutsu and focused on physical development and scientific fighting. He named it "judo," the supple way.

Kano also showed shrewdness when it came to presenting and promoting his new system. He used the government relationships he had developed as member of the educational board of Japan to push judo as part of the physical education curriculum of schools across Japan. Realizing that some type of encouragement should be given to students as they progressed through the ranks, he copied it from the traditional board game of Go, which consisted of 10 levels of mastery or *dan*; achievement of the first *dan* (*shodan*) was symbolized by changing the white practice belt for a black belt.[1]

Kano also created a standard uniform for students to wear. Before, judo practitioners, as well as any other martial arts students, had trained in street clothes. The new uniform, called *judogi* or *Gi*, had a double purpose: it was made of material resistant to all the pulling and stretching that vigorous practice required, and it also erased distinctions of class and wealth between students within the practice hall.

---

[1] J. Clements. 2016. *A Brief History of the Martial Arts*. London: Robinson.

The widespread popularity of judo was formally established in 1964, after Kano's death, when it became an Olympic sport. The idea had in fact been circling since the 1920s, but despite his keenness in promoting the style, Kano was surprisingly indifferent to the prospect and voiced his opinion in a way that left clear how he saw the method he had founded:

> My view on the matter [of judo becoming an Olympic sport], at present, is rather passive. If it be the desire of other member countries, I have no objection. But I do not feel inclined to take any initiative. For one thing, judo in reality is not a mere sport or game. I regard it as a principle of life, art and science. In fact, it is a means for personal cultural attainment. Only one of the forms of judo training, the so-called randori can be classed as a form of sport.

The Science of Judo

Judo is a fighting system that relies on using the strength of the adversary to gain control by applying the concept of "maximum efficiency with minimum effort." Both during drilling practice and in competition, most of its movements start from a standing position, where opponents grab each other's sleeve and lapel and try to unbalance and throw the other person to the ground.

In competition, points are awarded depending on how clearly the technique is executed. A clean throw means an automatic victory, but if it fails and both competitors go to the ground or if one of them manages to turn the body before hitting the mat, the match continues and the objective changes. Now the winner is the one who submits the opponent either by restraining him or her with both shoulders touching the mat or by forcing him or her to surrender via one of three methods:

1. Asphyxiation by cutting the flow of oxygen in the throat.
2. Strangulation by cutting the flow of blood through the neck.
3. Joint pressure to the limbs.

Being able to apply these techniques in a resisting, dynamic opponent requires a long learning process. Judo practitioners, also known as *judoka*, must first learn how to fall without injury. The judo practice hall uses soft mats for this purpose, but damage is still possible if thrown energetically, so judokas learn how to roll and how to position their bodies so they can fall repeatedly without harm.

Another area that requires intensive study is the catalog of throws and submissions. Judo is a scientific discipline, which relies not on intrinsic muscular power (although this is more relevant between equally trained practitioners than the principles of judo would indicate) but on the knowledge of the principles of balance and biomechanics used to gain control of the adversary. The extensive syllabus of judo includes:

- 67 throwing techniques divided into hand, hip, and leg throws as well as "sacrifice" throws.
- 30 grappling techniques divided into chokes, matholds, and joint locks.

The same as with karate, many of these movements are counterintuitive, and getting the judoka's body to apply them almost instinctively comes as a result of years of training and mechanical repetition.

Judo's Business Learnings for the Analyst

The applications of judo strategies to business success are very closely related to the principles that lie at the heart of the art as a flexible and scientific fighting style. Three of them are especially relevant when talking about the analytical behavioral style because of how well they align with its methodical nature.

1. Positioning and Movement

   In judo, victory is the result of a strategic plan, which depends on moving into the correct positioning. At the start of each bout, both practitioners are in a stable, secure stance. When one of them initiates the attack, he is putting himself out of balance as he generates momentum, and for an instant, he is vulnerable to counterattack. The only way the other judoka can take advantage of that window of opportunity is if he has previously moved to a position from where he can respond. As with a chess game, victory in judo comes when one of the fighters can exploit any failed maneuver made by the opponent. If the judoka cannot react in time, the opportunity passes, the opponent regains balance, and both return to the starting position.

The analyst behavior is notorious for its slow movement and long reaction times. The ingestion and processing of data are time-consuming, and the analyst is not comfortable issuing an opinion until they have been completed. The analyst can, however, develop a set of techniques that allow him or her to be as prepared as possible by practicing rapid movement and proper positioning. In a business environment, this does not mean physical movement but developing a default stance for those emergency cases where a quick response is necessary. This will act as a temporary measure of control and will provide the analyst time to develop a complete strategy.

2. Flexibility

Flexibility is such an essential concept to judo that it is incorporated in the very name of the discipline. Flexibility, as it is understood in judo practice, comes in two forms:

a. Conceptual flexibility: Refers to the core judo axiom of using the opponent's strength in your favor, giving way to superior force so it is directed in the manner you prefer. Giving way to the assault of that force causes it to become unbalanced in a way that can be controlled from a point of pivot.

b. Flexibility in execution: Refers to the ability to adjust a technique to a specific situation while maintaining in place the core principles that make it work. This allows to make adjustments based on variables like location, distance, timing, mass, and speed.

One of the big disadvantages of the analytical behavioral style is an inherent lack of flexibility; the analyst is defined by setting up a framework of rules and standards, which provide a solid foundation for this type of formal, task-oriented behavior. However, this comes at the cost of reducing the adaptability to unforeseen changes and sudden upsets of the environment. The same as with judokas, analyst businesspeople need to include a degree of flexibility in their character, allowing for deviation from regulations when an opportunity calls for it. This is also a way to diminish friction when working with behavioral types of the informal persuasion like the supporter or the promoter, who may find the analyst's adherence to guidelines too stifling.

Increased flexibility in the analyst's business applications could mean:

- Systematically looking at every issue from an additional point of view that is not based on data for alternative approaches.
- Evaluating project outcomes based not only on specific results but also on intangible business impact (team motivation, client/partner satisfaction, overall branding, etc.)
- Allowing for deviance from the established process in certain qualified cases.

3. Leverage

From a biomechanical perspective, the movements in most judo throwing techniques are divided into three stages:

a. *Tsukuri*, or the set of movements made in preparation to unbalance the opponent (by using both positioning and movement, as seen under "Positioning and Movement").

b. *Kuzushi*, or the action of actually unbalancing the opponent (by giving way in a flexible manner, as seen under "Flexibility").

c. *Kake*, or the actual execution of the throw using leverage.

It is at this last stage that the judoka turns the initiative of the opponent into his own by either selecting a point of pivot to turn his own body into an obstacle or sweeping the opponent's point of balance from under him. And depending where this point of pivot takes place, judo categorizes its techniques into three types:

- *Te waza* are the techniques that use arms, shoulders, or hands.
- *Koshi waza* are the techniques that use the hips, usually by lowering the judoka center of gravity and raising it to roll the opponent.
- *Ashi waza* are the techniques that use legs and feet.

Just as it is easier to open a door using a crowbar or lift a heavy object using a lever, the judoka acts as a fulcrum to move the opponent. Leverage, therefore, is understood as the point when the judoka undermines the opponent's attack and changes the course of action.

Similarly, the analyst's leverage comes from his or her organized disposition and reliance on data, very powerful tools in the modern world but which can also lead to inflexibility and unresponsiveness if not used properly. The lesson to be applied from judo into the analytical business style is to select the moment when those strengths come into play to change the flow of business. For example, when bidding for new clients, the analyst can leverage his or her organizational and data-driven abilities in three stages during the process:

Before	During	After
Strategy	People	Performance
Prove the adventages and value proposition of the offer versus competitors.	Assign ownership. Bring transparency and accountability to the business process	Analyze results and improve processes based on learnings.

Ultimately, the analyst can adopt from judo the lesson that Jigoro Kano promoted most eagerly. Since its conception, he envisioned the new martial art as a system of personal development, which was not reliant on aggressive movement but rather on a reactive and methodical cancellation of the assailant's attacks. As a fighting method, judo does not work well when the judoka tries to initiate the action. Similarly, the analyst can learn to embrace the characteristics that define his or her behavioral style and understand that a lack of proactivity is not a negative trait and that well-timed responsiveness can be equally effective.

CHAPTER 7

Learning from the Classics

Romance of the Three Kingdoms

A Book of Constant Influence

Sun Tzu's *Art of War* may be the title that most commonly comes to mind when talking about Chinese classic strategy treatises, but there is another book far more relevant to the modern business environment due both to its complexity and to the relativity of its moral approach.

The *Romance of the Three Kingdoms* is one of the four classic Chinese literary works (the others are the romantic *Dream of the Red Chamber*, the swashbuckling *The Water Margin*, and the adventurous *Travel to the West*) and was written by Luo Guanzhong between the years 1350 and 1400.

Its influence in Chinese culture cannot be sufficiently emphasized; paintings of the loyalty oath performed by the three main characters hang in the offices of CEOs and media tycoons. In 1938, Mao Zedong, future chairman of the Chinese Communist Party, made a rather grandiose statement to his ragtag group of guerrilla fighters, where he declared that the three-way conflict that engulfed China between him, the nationalist army of Chiang Kai-shek, and the invading Japanese imperial army was "like that of the Three Kingdoms."

While the *Art of War* is a dry and exhaustive listing of military strategies, addressing each possible situation a general may face, Luo Guanzhong's work takes a less obvious approach and disguises its martial lessons within a narrative context where they can be analyzed in detail, together with their consequences.

The book itself is a historical novel of great complexity with over one hundred and twenty chapters, almost one million words, and about one thousand characters. It describes in dramatized form events that took place during the period of Chinese history known as The Three Kingdoms, between the years of 220 and 265 AD.

Set during the reign of the Han dynasty, imperial power is waning and corruption and political instability prompt the rise of local warlords and different military factions. Some are aimed at maintaining the imperial status quo, some others try to replace it, while yet others plan to use the chaotic circumstances to establish new centers of power through the kingdom. At the turning point of the novel, the weakness of Han military power is made evident when it fails to repress the Yellow Turban religious sect uprising. In a desperate attempt to restore order, the emperor recruits a large number of warlords, but when commanded to disband after the war by the weakened central government, several of the mercenary armies pay no heed.

Eventually, three different kingdoms emerge from the remains of the Han Empire and become the main actors in the ongoing fight for power, engulfed in a narrative that spans decades.

- The kingdom of Wu, which is under the leadership of Sun Quan.
- The kingdom of Shu, which is governed by Liu Bei. Liu Bei is arguably the main character in the novel; an archetypical Chinese folk hero, he is learned, intelligent, and has a personality deeply rooted in a type of humanism that is ruled by the traditional Confucian doctrines. He precipitates the events of the novel by forming a brotherhood in the famous Peach Tree Garden ceremony with the

other two main characters of the book: Guan Yu, the moral adviser, and Zang Fei, the legendary warrior. Liu Bei's objective is to restore the Han Dynasty, with which he has blood ties, to its former power, and he strives to do so throughout the novel. He boasts outstanding skills in managing human resources and often succeeds in putting the right person in the right position, developing, in turn, his power base.

- The kingdom of Wei, which is ruled by Cao Cao. Originally, Cao Cao emerges as the main antagonist to Liu Bei and as the villain of the story: a political animal of tyrannical behavior. But his natural abilities (courage, discipline) and personality make him a more complex and admirable character as the narrative progresses. His impact on Chinese culture has extended outside literature to become an archetypical persona that appears even on the stage of Chinese opera performances, where the Cao character wears a distinctive white mask to suggest treacherousness and cunning. Cao Cao is ultimately in the defeated party of the Red Cliff battle, one of the most famous military conflicts in Chinese history.

Once all three rulers have declared themselves kings, there follows a series of struggles, where the borders of the territory held by each of the warring factions weave back and forth for years among personal and political intrigues.

The period of the Three Kingdoms eventually ends, not with the triumph of Liu Bei and his supporters, but with the unification of China under the new Jin dynasty: a pattern that reinforces the cyclical character of Chinese history and highlights the importance of the opening sentence of the book: "The Empire, long divided, must unite; long united, must divide. Thus it has ever been."

Modern-Day Relevance of *Romance* of the *Three Kingdoms*

The novel is, at its heart, a compendium of Confucian values, and it is the adherence to these, or lack thereof, that serves to distinguish between heroes and villains in the story. Each character is identified with one or several Confucian virtues or morally repudiated vices.

- Cao Cao = Ambition, decisiveness, talent
- Liu Bei = Tolerance and humanism
- Zhuge Liang = Loyalty and diligence
- Lü Bu = Betrayal and lust

But beyond classical values, the book holds immense learnings for the business world and serves as a model for developing professional and leadership skills. Particularly relevant are the questions posed around the following areas:

a) The planning of strategic action
    Which action should I take? What is my value proposition?
b) The management of human resources
    Who can I rely on? How can I attract talent?
c) The development of personal relationships
    Who should I ally myself with? Who can I support and who can support me?

The chaotic and destructive environment that serves as a background in *Romance of the Three Kingdoms* can be compared to the confusion of the business world, and the behavior of the different antagonists in the novel offers keys to understand the actions of business partners and rivals in real life.

Three strategies appear again and again as the most effective in addressing the questions of strategic action, resource management, and relationship building:

Strategies to Survive in a Turbulent Environment ("Fishing in Troubled Waters")

Complex business environments tend to generate a great amount of frustration for business leaders. This can happen in any country and in any industry, but developing markets (Southeast Asia, Latin America, Africa), in general, and China, in particular, have been a particularly good example in the last decade and a half because of the large revenue opportunity they represent.

The market in China is a convoluted mix of local small firms, overseas conglomerates looking for a foothold, and domestic juggernauts steamrolling their resources into a particular opportunity. Numerous foreign companies with a large amount of overseas presence look to capitalize on the business opening and, in doing so, collide with strong local companies engaged in rapid growth. For the foreign businessperson, this may seem like a chaotic situation, and many cannot help but wonder how much of this is by accident and how much is by design.

In *Romance of the Three Kingdoms*, this scenario is the norm; different factions seek to alter the normal social status and, in the ensuing confusion, gain positions of advantage against major rivals, a principle they define under the name "fishing in troubled waters." Chinese companies apply the "create disorder to survive" mentality in the business arena for the same reason, and as a result, the market becomes unpredictable both in the actions of companies and in the reaction of consumers (price wars, irregular behavior, sudden expansions, etc.). The situation is further aggravated by institutional influence and poor or changing state regulations.

Fortunately, one solution to this is also offered in the pages of the novel. *Romance of the Three Kingdoms* explains that everything is cyclical: if a situation of stability starts to deteriorate, it will be followed by one of unbalance. But as soon as the confusion climaxes, an opposite effect gets under way. Any unbalanced status quo is resolved when it naturally forces the chaotic and weak elements out of the process, and what results is a renewed stable state headed by new factions and players.

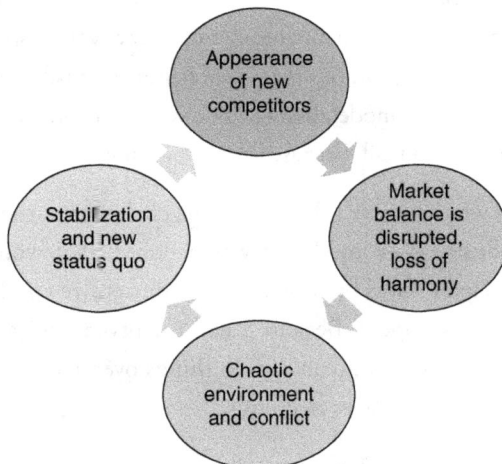

The creation of a turbulent environment for an enterprise does not depend only on external factors. Companies have to make fundamental decisions that deal with their identity, how they approach their growth, and how they invest in resources. Hiroshi Mikitani, founder of the Internet Japanese giant Rakuten, often refers to the "War model" versus the "Combat model" when doing business, and he uses a *Romance of the Three Kingdoms* analogy to explain his theory:

> The overall strategy that I formulated was to expand the company's performance in this manner. Through a gradual accumulation of victories, we eventually reached a critical point, and then we switched the strategy over to the war business model.
>
> If we wanted to sound cool, perhaps we could call it the style of Liu Bei, a character in the Three Kingdoms Saga. It is an old story set in ancient China. The formation of Liu Bei's army began when a pledge of brotherhood was made between his friends, Guan Yu and Zhang Fei. This meant that their "army" consisted of only three people at first.
>
> By going to war in China during its period of conflict, and getting more and more victories under their belts (although they were defeated many times), they were able in a short period of time to build up a considerable military force, and ultimately establish a single, united country, called Shuhan.
>
> Under the war business model—the model where from the beginning you make large investments and have a big army at your disposal—the return for success is great, but the risk of failure is equally great. With the combat business model, like Liu Bei, you can easily pick yourself up again, even if you fail, because there is nothing much to lose.
>
> The reason why we were able to meet the challenge of the Internet shopping business—a model, it was believed, that would never succeed in Japan—was because from the outset, we employed the combat business model. Because I had the psychological fallback of knowing that we could always do things over again, I was able to make bold and decisive decisions.[1]

---

[1] H. Mikitani. 2007. *Principles for Success*. Tokyo.

Strategies to Solve the Apparent Contradiction in Fundamental Values and Real Tactical Behavior[2]

In *Romance of the Three Kingdoms*, characters from different factions betray each other and shift alliances in a way that seems Machiavellian to the reader and particularly deplorable to Western mentalities. Even when professing feelings of loyalty and duty, the warlords of the novel don't hesitate to attach each other's armies, pillage resources, and, right after, go back to lofty declamations about brotherly devotion and fealty.

Any human interaction, be it between individuals or groups, can be the victim of a fundamental flaw: the need for practicality. Often, principles of correct behavior held by all participants suddenly disappear when it comes to the reality of their actions and the need to make moral concessions. This dichotomy, when present in the business process, produces the following pairings:

Fundamental values	Tactical behavior
Loyalty/responsibility	Convenience
Common good	Personal benefit
Honesty	Deception
Harmony	Disorder

An in-depth reading of *Romance of the Three Kingdoms* offers an internal logic to these actions, which is dictated by the warring landscape where the relationships take place. The novel explains the apparent contradiction between fundamental values and their external expression by way of the "buffer zone" theory. It assumes that every actor protects himself or herself from harm by establishing an area of security that keeps unknown newcomers at arm's length. While the core behavior of the actor is regulated by a set of morally correct traditional values, these stay tucked away at the center of the buffer zone. The zone itself acts as protective measure and is set in place to (a) identify allies and (b) to protect the actor from more powerful enemies. A newcomer can end up establishing a relationship of trust with the actor, one that is ruled by humanistic values, but, to achieve this, he or she must first sort through the filtering system

---

[2]L. Yan, and T. Hafsi. 2007. *Understand Chinese Business Behavior: A Historical Perspective from Three Kingdoms to Modern China.* Montréal, QC: HEC Montreal.

of the buffer zone that can take different shapes, including duplicity, disinformation, and ambiguity.

There are two specific examples of how this theory of the buffer zone works in the novel:

1. Guan Yu was one of the generals serving under the hero Liu Bei. When captured by his enemy, Cao Cao, out of respect for his skills, he was offered the opportunity to work for Cao Cao's banner in exchange for his life. Guan Yu accepted under strict conditions, which included the right to return to his liege lord if the opportunity presented itself. When this finally happened, Cao Cao allowed him to leave as promised and Guan joined Liu Bei's army again.
   - None of the two leaders, Liu Bei or Cao Cao, saw the general's behavior as traitorous. In fact, Cao Cao managed to push through Guan Yu's buffer zone and reached a state of "cordial opposition" where balance could be achieved.
   - It can be argued that Guan Yu acted as bridge between the two factions and helped, in the long term, to reduce chaos in the country.
2. The young general Lu Xun besieged the city of Jingzhou, which was defended by Guan Yu. In order to establish negotiations, Lu Xun wrote a letter of great humility, which praised his opponent. But while doing so, Lu Xun had ordered his soldiers to dress up as merchants and take the city. Lu Xun's maneuver worked well but debased him in the eyes of Guan Yu, creating a long-term relationship of animosity.
   - Although militarily speaking the tactic was correct, it resulted in a short-term gain, which lowered Lu Xun's standing with his opponent, Guan Yu.
   - Lu Xun's behavior failed to pass the buffer zone established by Guan Yu, and both actors remained in violent opposition, which, in turn, extended the conflict and increased chaos in the country.

In China's current business environment, such ambiguity is constantly present. Many foreign companies find frustrating what they consider the untrustworthiness of the local players and the duplicitousness of their word compared to their actions. But seen from the filter of the learnings in *Romance of the Three Kingdoms*, such local companies are merely adopting the buffer zone strategy, perhaps by design, perhaps in an unconscious manner, to protect themselves from overseas actors.

Furthermore, large enterprises entering a new market like China often show attitudes that are actually considered aggressive from the local perspective. Approaches such as being interested in immediate benefits without true commitment to the market, arriving with an overwhelming strategic and resource superiority, or even making explicit declarations about the intention to fully dominate an industry will create friction because, from a local company's perspective, such behavior can be qualified as untrustworthy. Additionally, big foreign corporations trying to consolidate a position of power without respecting the overall balance of the market exhibit a selfish behavior if they don't try to establish alliances with other companies.

As a result, the relationships between local players and overseas newcomers are stuck in the antagonistic buffer zone, and neither of them gets the opportunity to develop beyond that state of shared mistrust.

Strategies for the Recurrent Usage of Deception Tactics to Gain Advantage

Tactical behavior is an aggregation of many different skills, and one of them, frequently seen in the novel, is that of deception. Offering "misinformation" or confusing clues and hiding one's real intentions helps an actor because it

- Creates time to consider and evaluate the intentions of the other party
- Gives an opportunity to analyze the sincerity of any offer received and filter allies from enemies
- Allows a degree of self-protection by hiding the actor's own strengths and weaknesses while assessing the other party

The obvious, most simplistic purpose when using deception tactics is to deceive the other party, but at a more elaborate level, they can be a tool that helps, if properly applied, to establish a basis for a relationship of trust.

There are, again, two specific examples of how deception applied to a higher strategic objective works in the novel:

1. A good example of this tactic in action is the initial relationship between the two main characters in *Romance of the Three Kingdoms*. Zhue Liang, the adviser par excellence, puts himself at the service of the hero Liu Bei, but to Liu Bei's surprise, he initially shows little respect and deference toward his new lord. Liu Bei understands that having Zhue Liang is a great asset and sets aside his personal pride for the sake of his faction. Using great patience and restraint, he shows to the strategist that he is an enlightened leader, working for the good of the land. Thus convinced, Zhue Liang offers his unconditional support, and the kingdom of Shu gains the benefit of his skills.
   - Zhue Liang's attitude was indeed a tactic of deception created for the purpose of testing Liu Bei's values.
2. This approach is in stark contrast to the one the villain Cao Cao uses. When offended by his capable minister, My Heng, Cao Cao reacts by having him promptly executed.
   - Cao Cao, unable to put aside personal feelings, does not dig deeper in order to evaluate the reasons behind My Heng's behavior and reacts impulsively. As a result, he loses the contribution of an efficient adviser, but also, this reaction warns other ministers, who quickly leave him.

Such deception tactics, similar to the use of the buffer zone, are, in the novel, protective measures rather than a sign of malicious behavior, and their objective is to level the field so smaller players can compete with larger ones. The single most effective way to overcome them is by establishing balance and harmony.

The final piece of advice for global companies frustrated by the confusion of local markets, be it in China or somewhere else, would be the same that appears in *Romance of the Three Kingdoms*:

- Think and behave in terms of commitment, looking to develop long-term relationships.

- Establish effective communication with local players.
- Create social capital (a relationship network) not as an object of transaction or interest but as a compendium of reciprocal obligations.
- Do not hesitate to establish relationships of competitiveness with local entities but make sure they are accompanied with relationships of cooperation.

Although some of these principles may sound vague and even wishful, the real impact they have should not be overlooked. In 1992, AIG was the first foreign insurance company allowed to develop business in mainland China, while others had to wait until 2000, eight more years, before getting the same treatment. The company attributed this, partially, to the Chinese government's acknowledgment of its commitment to the country since it was the only overseas insurer to remain in China after the Japanese occupation of 1936.

Liu Bei would have recognized the gesture.

CHAPTER 8

The Promoter Style

CEO Use Case: Steve Jobs, a Born Promoter

In his 2011 biography of Steve Jobs, journalist and writer Walter Isaacson made continuous references to three characteristics in the personality of the founder and most charismatic CEO of Apple. First was just how much a difficult person Jobs was to work with; there are a large number of stories and anecdotes about the thin, tall man yelling at employees and partners while piercing them with his unsettling stare. The second characteristic, which may seem contradictory, was his supernatural ability to motivate the people around him and push them beyond their apparent limit. The third characteristic was his outstanding capability as a communicator. Jobs is still considered by many as the greatest corporate narrator there ever was, based on his ability to engage audiences with his vision of simple, powerful, and elegant products.

These traits would often coalescence into something that Apple employees called the "Jobs Reality Distortion Field." Named after a science fiction story where aliens create an alternative reality by using their mental force, Jobs seemed equally able to, by sheer force of will, change the conditions of the world around himself and convince others that his vision, contradictory to circumstances as it may seem, was the correct one. Even at the conception of the company and still a young man, Jobs pushed his friend and Apple's cofounder, Steve Wozniak, to complete in 4 days a computer program he had estimated would take months to prepare. Despite Wozniak's initial reticence, he was compelled by the absolute certainty his friend irradiated.[1]

Isaacson includes in his book a similar anecdote about the "Jobs Reality Distortion Field":

> One day, Jobs marched into the cubicle of Larry Kenyon, the engineer who was working on the Macintosh operating system, and complained that it was taking too long to boot up. Kenyon started to explain why reducing the boot-up time wasn't possible, but Jobs cut him off. "If it would save a person's life, could you find a way to shave 10 seconds off the boot time?" he asked. Kenyon allowed that he probably could. Jobs went to a whiteboard and showed that if five million people were using the Mac and it took 10 seconds extra to turn it on every day, that added up to 300 million or so hours a year—the equivalent of at least 100 lifetimes a year. After a few weeks Kenyon had the machine booting up 28 seconds faster.[2]

It is interesting to note that neither in this description nor in any of the others Isaacson includes in his book did Jobs tell his team how to accomplish what he was asking for; he just demanded results.

Outside of Apple, Jobs's powers of persuasion were also legendary. The most quoted part of his 2007 iPhone launch presentation showcases the depth of his promotional skills:

> Today, we're introducing three revolutionary products. The first one is a widescreen iPod with touch controls. The second is a revolutionary mobile phone. And the third is a breakthrough internet communications device. So, three things: a widescreen iPod with touch controls; a revolutionary mobile phone; and a breakthrough

---

[1]W. Isaacson. 2012. "The Real Leadership Lessons of Steve Jobs." *Harvard Business Review*. https://hbr.org/2012/04/the-real-leadership-lessons-of-steve-jobs
[2]W. Isaacson. 2007. "Steve Jobs."

internet communications device. An iPod, a phone, and an internet communicator. An iPod, a phone—are you getting it? These are not three separate devices. This is one device, and we are calling it...iPhone.

Today Apple is going to reinvent the phone.

In all these episodes, there are two patterns of behavior exhibited by Jobs repeatedly.

1. He had a vision. Jobs's basic formulation for all Apple products was based on providing a flawless consumer experience via (a) simplicity, (b) efficiency, and (c) design. During his conversations with both internal and external audiences, he would issue demands or promote values, but he would always refer back to the underlying vision in order to anchor his ideas.
2. He used emotion to share that vision. Jobs was as famous for his quick temper and scant patience as he was for his passionate product presentations. When it came to chastising and, on occasions, praising his employees, he did not use a logical approach to evaluate their performance. Similarly, when engaging the market, he appealed to the audience sense of wonder by using storytelling techniques, humor, and surprises.

Both internally in Apple and externally in the market, Jobs was a born augur for his business, tirelessly driving his vision forward and engaging his audience at an emotional level. From a behavioral perspective, he falls squarely into a highly energetic, driven, and charismatic business style: the promoter.

The Bases of the Promoter Behavioral Style

The promoter behavioral style belongs to a dynamic and motivating type of person who places emphasis on big ideas. This is a style often seen in politics and entertainment, where charisma and smooth communication skills can be used to influence and persuade others. Government figures like Bill Clinton, TV personalities like Oprah Winfrey and Jay Leno, and actors like Will Smith have all been classified as promoters in the past.

The same as with the supporter behavioral style, the promoter displays an informal, people-oriented alignment, and it is this informality that makes them socially outgoing and friendly. But while the supporter has genuine interest in others from a human perspective, the promoter takes a more utilitarian approach and looks to gain influence in pursuit of specific goals or get approval from those they admire.

The promoter is doubtlessly the most enjoyable type of person to be around; he or she has creative imagination and excels in motivating groups to work toward a common goal. Where the controller does this via example and stern direction, the promoter has a softer touch, and their competitive spirits are collaborative rather than abrasive.

At its extreme, this type of behavior can become boasting or careless, jumping ahead to conclusions too rapidly. The promoter is not given to detailed analysis and can easily make generalizations that miss the mark. The promoter's freeflowing nature often benefits from working with styles like the analyst or the controller, the two formal-leaning styles that focus on planning and structure, where the visionary aspect of the promoter fits well with the more down-to-earth approach the analyst and controller provide. If put under pressure, the promoter's initial reaction would be to try and talk his or her way out of trouble, and on occasions, the promoter may throw a tantrum in order to escape a difficult situation.

In any event, the biggest asset the promoter style brings to a work environment is the promoter's creativeness and expressiveness. He or she can help a team or organization to constantly keep in mind the bigger picture and define both the business value they provide and their corporate identity.

The Promoter at the Table: Negotiation and Communication Style

The promoter is an innate salesperson, a prophet, and a guru all rolled into one. His or her default position when communicating is that of persuasion: trying to get others to share their point of view and, often, doing this in a charming way. The promoter is a highly sociable person who prefers to solve any existing issues by engaging in direct communication rather than drafting charts and memos. His or her capability to connect through many relationships may be seen as insincere by others, especially because the promoter can be selective in the connections they grows, developing more those that provide greater value.

During negotiations, the promoter can drive a hard bargain, but he or she does so in such an alluring way that it seems they are conceding on all points.

When communicating with the promoter, it is important to keep in mind that he or she generally has genuine interest in including points of view from others but may be derailed by their own vision. Making sure they look at issues from multiple aspects will help the communication process.

The biggest flaw of the promoter is his or her carelessness when dealing with details. A way to smooth a working relationship with them is by making sure (supervising them if necessary) that they have prepared and done their homework and by making them accountable for working through the muncane, mechanical tasks. Otherwise, there is a risk that decisions are made based on intuition with no facts supporting them.

The Promoter at the Helm: Leadership Style

While the other proactive behavioral style, the controller, is driven to win, the promoter finds that is not enough; the promoter wants to win and to do it in style. They have penchant for showmanship that fuels their popularity and prestige. The reason for this is that the source of authority for the promoter does not come from their technical or specialize knowledge, not even from his or her business savviness. Instead, the promoter is a leader by force of conviction and self-image.

The leadership style of the promoter can be relentless and puts great pressure on his or her team, but because it comes articulated around an inspirational style, it is readily accepted. As a result, the promoter will tend to focus on the positive outlook of things regardless of how dire they may be and will rally the troops around themselves and provide direction. Such enthusiasm may not change the nature or size of the problem, but it is contagious in a way that makes the task seem more meaningful.

The promoter leader is willing to take risks and aim for bigger prizes. This is partially due to his or her ambitious nature but, also, to the way he or she enjoys the excitement of fast-paced environments. Working under a promoting behavioral-style type of manager requires someone to buy into and share the grand vision and ultimate goals the leader sets, in order to endure the tougher aspects of the job.

The Promoter: Relationships Chart

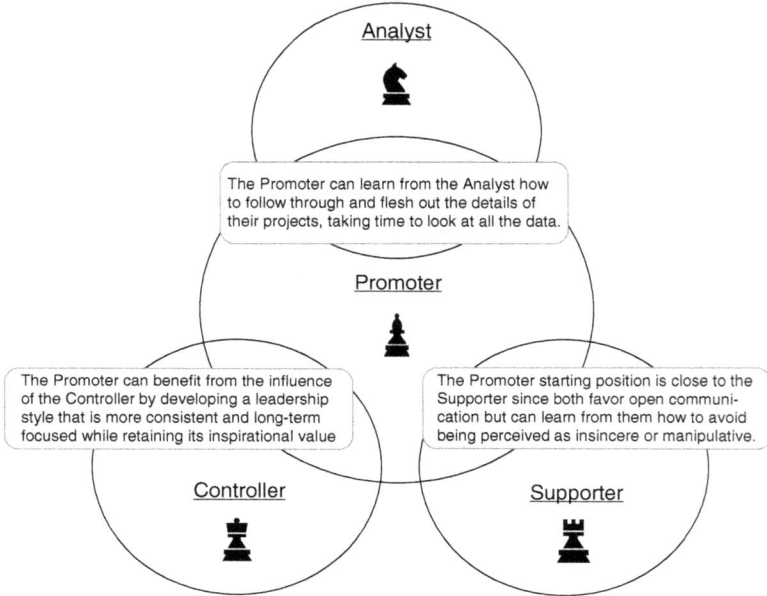

Analyst

The Promoter can learn from the Analyst how to follow through and flesh out the details of their projects, taking time to look at all the data.

Promoter

The Promoter can benefit from the influence of the Controller by developing a leadership style that is more consistent and long-term focused while retaining its inspirational value

The Promoter starting position is close to the Supporter since both favor open communication but can learn from them how to avoid being perceived as insincere or manipulative.

Controller

Supporter

CHAPTER 9

Mixed Martial Arts (MMA)

The Promoting Fighting Style

The Origins of Mixed Martial Arts

In 1964, two practitioners of Chinese martial arts met at a training studio in the city of Oakland, California. The fight was scheduled for late evening and was to take place behind closed doors with just seven people as spectators. In the larger scheme of things, it was an inconsequential affair and would have been promptly forgotten if one of the two 23-year-olds who fought that day had not been Bruce Lee.

The man who would become an actor known worldwide, launch the "Kung Fu craze" of the early 1970s, and eventually become synonymous with martial arts was not just an on-screen performer. His ability and continuous dedication to fighting, from its most practical aspects to the philosophical implications of unarmed combat as a way of self-expression and identity, was very real, and, by the time he died at age 32, he had spent more than a decade trying to create and refine the ultimate fighting syllabus.

Although raised in Hong Kong, Lee was actually born in San Francisco and had a U.S. passport. He moved to Seattle in 1959 at age 18 and enrolled in the University of Washington, where he started teaching martial art classes to a heterogeneous group of friends and students. Since he was never a tournament competitor, it is hard to gauge actually how good he would have been as a professional fighter, but he led a turbulent life as a young man in Hong Kong, and there are reports of gang fights on rooftops and in back alleys during his teenage years.

By the time he arrived to the West Coast, Lee was a practitioner of one specific type of Chinese martial art (known as Wushu, or more popularly, kung fu), in particular, the Wing Chun boxing form, which he had learned from his Hong Kong teacher, Ip Man. Lee's activities as a trainer in the United States soon became polemic; he criticized other forms of traditional Chinese Martial Arts as stiff, obsolete, and ineffective. In the inaugural Long Beach martial arts Tournament that took place in 1964, Lee did not compete. Instead, he took center stage to perform a demonstration of his technique, and, again, he used the occasion to launch a tirade that left much of the Californian fighting community—and especially the San Francisco's Chinatown schools of kung fu—upset about this young upstart. In their view, Lee, despite possessing some obvious skill, had done nothing to prove that his style was more effective than other, more established ones.

At this point, Lee was at a crossroads. He could sense that traditional martial art styles that relied on forms and passive training marked by solo drills could not prevail over active, efficiency-focused workouts with live sparring and resistant opponents. But he was not certain that his own style of Wing Chun, although simple, streamlined, and direct, was actually the solution he was searching for.

The man he fought that evening in Oakland was a Chinese northern-style expert called Wong Jack Man, who had made a reputation for himself in San Francisco as an accomplished, if somewhat traditional, martial arts master.

Legend has it that Wong Jack Man was directed by the Chinatown elders to challenge Lee because he was teaching Chinese martial arts to Westerners and somehow revealing traditional secrets, but most researchers think the reason was far more prosaic and it was linked to Lee's bravado. As Lee's wife, Linda Lee, later stated, "Only Bruce and Man know why they fought."[1] There exist several versions of what happened and how the fight developed. Some describe it as a movie-like choreography of punches and kicks, but reality seems to have been more mundane, and, according, again, to Lee's wife, Linda, both men chased each other around the room with little regard for complicated techniques and acrobatics until they grappled and fell to the floor and Lee pounded Wong Jack Man with punches while shouting, "Do you give up?" between gulps of ragged breath.

---

[1]C. Russo. 2016. *Striking Distance: Bruce Lee and the Dawn of Martial Arts in America.* Lincoln, NE: University of Nebraska Press.

What we know for certain is that, after that fight, Lee was extremely disappointed with himself. He had not won—if indeed he did—as effortlessly or as decisively as he had expected. His physical condition had failed him. His technique had failed him. From that moment on, he moved away from his traditional style and spent nearly 10 years looking for something more effective: a combination of techniques that were not bogged down by static forms and conventions. He researched extensively different fighting methods: boxing; wrestling; fencing; as well as Chinese, Korean, and Japanese martial arts, looking to incorporate all that which worked into a new fighting method. A mixed martial art of sorts.

The Hybrid Nature of Mixed Martial Arts

There is a certain consensus that if Bruce Lee had not died at the age of 32 in 1973, the evolution he had started would have soon resulted in the fighting style we now know as Mixed Martial Arts (MMA). However, in Lee's absence, the birth was prolonged, and the official start of MMA is normally given as November 12, 1993: the first UFC event.

This Ultimate Fighting Championship, or UFC, started that year as a tournament, with modified rules created to determine which fighting form was the most effective. Many other promotions have been created since, but it is the blend of styles that fighters adopted in order to effectively compete in the UFC that would eventually be known as MMA.

MMA, rather than a martial art per se, is a construct of different fighting formats integrated into one smooth, high-performance-oriented system. By "performance-oriented," the understanding is that MMA is designed and practiced to win fights in the ring or the cage—an octagonal enclosure built to avoid the shortcomings of the boxing ring when grappling and wrestling are involved[2]—and has no forms or *kata* nor any other meditational aspects present in traditional martial arts.

---

[2] The octagonal shape offers more open corners than a square ring, so fighters cannot be locked into an angle with no escape. The use of wire fence as opposed to ropes prevents fighters from falling or being thrown out of the arena and into the public.

Although different fighters adapt a different mixture of techniques to their own taste, for most practitioners, the MMA form of combat incorporates the following catalog of movements:

- Striking, long distance: karate, taekwondo, or muay thai kicks.
- Striking, short distance: Boxing punches. karate or muay thai elbow and knee strikes.
- Grappling, standing: Wrestling or judo holds and throws.
- Grappling, ground: Wrestling or judo holds. Brazilian jiu jitsu submissions.

The other characteristic of MMA is the speed with which a fighter needs to transition from one style to another. This is actually where one of the biggest difficulties to master MMA appears; the skills necessary to become a good striker and a good grappler are very different and have to be developed separately. Only after reaching a high degree of proficiency in both can they be integrated in such a way that the shift from a standing attack position to a close-quarters clinch to the ground, and back up again, is performed seamlessly.

Due to its hybrid nature, MMA can incorporate dozens of different movements; some are very basic, while others are extremely specific to one of the source fighting styles, which makes it very difficult to present a comprehensive catalog of MMA techniques. But because of their proven effectiveness, there are several basic attacks that appear in every fight and form of the basic inventory of MMA fighting.

1. Jab/Cross (boxing). The straight punch to the face or body delivered from the left (jab) or right (cross) hand is the basic striking tool in the MMA arsenal. The linearity of jab and cross makes both of them fast attacks, while their use of body weight behind the arm powers a solid blow when hitting with proper timing and speed.
2. Round kick (muay thai/karate). The MMA round kick is thrown by pivoting the support leg at the time of kicking and adding the torsion of the hips to the mass of the leg to deliver power. The round kick is the preferred long-distance attack in MMA fights

and has a phenomenal reach and force. It can be thrown at three different levels, with an increasing degree of difficulty: low, mid, and high. The low kick targets the opponent's leg to hamper movement, the mid kick targets the torso to deplete stamina via trauma to liver and lungs, and, finally, the high kick aims for the head and a knockout.

3. Takedown (wrestling). The takedown is an attack where fighters use a level change to lower their stance and grab the hips or legs of the opponent to throw them to the ground. The takedown needs to be closely followed by a move to gain control over the prostrated opponent when reaching the ground in order to secure a dominant position.

4. Rear naked choke (Brazilian jiu jitsu). The rear naked choke is a strangulation technique where the fighter gets a dominant position at the back of the opponent and, using the forearm, applies pressure to the neck while holding his own biceps with the opposite hand to create leverage and increase force. Fighters often use strikes to create an opening in the opponent's guard in order to set up the rear naked choke.

5. Ground-and-pound (MMA). Ground-and-pound is the most characteristic MMA technique and the one most closely associated with the style; because of its mixture of striking and grappling, MMA is one of the very few combat sports where hitting from the ground is allowed. Ground-and-pound's most common application happens when, after taking down their opponent, fighters hold a top dominant mount position and attack using punches and elbow strikes while controlling the opponent's torso with knees and legs. Pressed against the floor and with little room for escape, an MMA fighter on the receiving end of the ground-and-pound position has little option but to surrender or be rendered unconscious.

MMA's Business Learnings for the Promoter

The technical applications of the moves that MMA uses are certainly original, but the techniques themselves are the same seen when reviewing karate, judo, or, later on, Brazilian jiu jitsu (BJJ). Because of that, the business learnings in this chapter do not come from martial arts practice; instead, MMA's insights for the corporate person are actually direct business lessons based on the revenue model of the professional MMA world.

Although there exists a solid amateur community, what sets MMA apart from other martial arts is the focus of professional fighters and promoters on developing the sport as a business-focused spectator sport. Similar to boxing, MMA looked from its inception to monetize itself in a high-revenue format, which combines the best of athletic competitions and show business.

Competitors are required to have an outstanding physical ability, but, while for judo or karate competitors that is enough to bring Olympic medals and world tournaments, a degree of promotional sense is integral to the success of an MMA fighter. This is because the opportunity to book events and win championships (and the prize money they include) is directly related to how entertaining their fights may be. Highly demanded fighters whom the public is eager to see get to monetize their events to a higher degree than similar, maybe equally accomplished, fighters who lack appeal.

Moreover, because the MMA professional fighting business makes promotional efforts an intrinsic part of their fighter compensation, those with more business acumen have a greater chance of multiplying their revenue sources—which are all directly linked to their fan support—via the following:

- Fight bonuses: Some incentives, like UFC's "Performance of the Night bonus" or "Fight of the Night bonus," can bring six-figure prize money for popular fighters.
- Pay-per-view revenue: The main revenue source, for the UFC and other MMA promotions, comes from TV paid subscription services. High-profile fights can surpass the million-mark subscriber order.
- Endorsement contracts: When a fighter reaches a certain level of popularity, multiple brands will offer endorsement opportunities for products ranging from athletic gear to energy drinks or video-game releases.

In short, showmanship, as well as fighting skill, has become a pivotal factor in the business of MMA fighting.

There are three specific learnings any businessperson can apply from the world of MMA but that are especially relevant to the promoter behavioral style. As leadership writer Allan Vayman[3] puts it:

> To casual observers the Ultimate Fighting Championship is little more than a brute contest. Blood and teeth spill on the Octagon. However what the organization has done to elevate the sport of mixed martial arts over the last 20 years is remarkable. . .and offers lesson for any startup executive.

> For a fighter to be top-ranked in his weight class, it requires a rare combination of natural ability, a cultivated arsenal of skills, and the heart to persevere against uber-talented competition. To all you entrepreneurs, is this ringing a bell?

> While most people will never know what it's like to step into the Octagon, as a spectator there are many parallels we can draw from our business lives.

Performance Is Important but It Is All about the Preparation Behind

This is hardly a novel notion, but the need to have a solid preparation for the task ahead is especially relevant in MMA. Because competition requires achieving a high degree of proficiency in multiple disciplines, many fighters spend decades training and may only have a single fight to prove they are worthy of making it to and competing in the highest paying leagues. Come fight night, their performance will depend on how well they react under pressure and bring forth the skills they have accumulated.

The nature of the promoter's behavioral style predisposes him or her to be comfortable in the spotlight, but also makes the promoter not as diligent as he or she could be in doing the proper groundwork. The promoter cannot, the same as the MMA fighter, rely only on talent to succeed at that crucial moment of truth. An MMA-like approach to preparation, which backs up that ambitious idea and allows it to

[3]A. Vayman. 2015. "What Every Entrepreneur Can Learn from UFC". *B2B News Network*. https://www.b2bnn.com/2015/02/every-entrepreneur-can-learn-ufc/

prosper means, for the promoter, the certainty that they will be able to deliver.

Focus on Doing Well What You Hate

Although the sport of MMA has evolved tremendously in the last decade and has increased in popular standing, many practitioners, rather than starting their career directly in the discipline, come incentivized by the challenge of competition and its economic rewards after years of training in other styles like Brazilian jiu jitsu, boxing, or wrestling. More often than not, these fighters have a background in one of the two large specialized combat fields: striking or wrestling. Although they need to become proficient in both to succeed, they will most likely favor that approach from where they originally developed, and overcoming that tendency is one of the main challenges if they are to master the wide range of skills required in competition at the highest level. MMA fighters are, therefore, famous for focusing on doing well the things they may not like. Strikers have to become good grapplers and wrestlers have to become efficient strikers.

The promoter behavioral style is energetic and active but is also selective. Promoters, because of their competitive spirit and creativity, do what they like well but have a difficult time diving deeper into the details that will make the grand, ambitious framework that they propose to come to fruition. The same as happens to MMA fighters, where adaptability is key to cover the fighter's weaker areas, the promoter must expand and improve:

- Using an analyst-like approach to data and scientific decision making, making sure things like budget and revenue returns will align to make the big idea work.
- Using controller-like attention to detail to confirm the resources are in place to complete the different tasks involved.
- Using a supporter-like engagement disposition to make sure their teams are sincerely involved in the project and that success depends on the effort of the whole group rather than one person.

For the promoter, the same as for the MMA fighter, focusing on doing what is difficult will ultimately drive better results.

The Lone Fighter Is Always Part of a Team

MMA is a combat sport, and as such, it is a lonely activity. At the end of the day, it is up to the fighter to step into the ring or the cage and wrestle a win away from the opponent with no other assistance than skill and training. But it takes a team to get there. At the higher levels of professional MMA fighting, competitors train specifically for a designed opponent. They engage in intensive training camps at least 2 months previous to the bout, where specialized coaches and training partners will analyze in detail the style of the adversary and try to find a weakness. Despite all their efforts and proficiency, fighters cannot prepare on their own; they are just the crucible where the talent of a whole team coalescences.

Similarly, because the promoter can be remiss in carrying out the specifics of the plan he or she had envisioned, having a solid support team is key. Those team members are the people who will make tangible the strategy, they will create the product, and they will design the code. For promoter personalities, there is the continuous risk that their rock star-like tendencies may alienate that team, either by pushing it too far or by hogging the limelight and not sharing the recognition of success.

The name of the MMA fighter is what appears in the promotional pieces and the newspaper headlines, but very few fail to recognize the team that supports them in getting there. Similarly, the promoter would benefit from understanding that his or her relationship with one's team flows in both equally important directions: They inspire a group and are, in turn, supported by it.

CHAPTER 10

Learning from the Classics

The Bubishi

Tracking the Legacy of the Bubishi

Before the widespread use of industrial technology applied to information—which started with the printing press, continues with modern digital channels, and allowed to quickly create identical copies of data packages (be it books, films, or files)—the biggest challenge related to the conservation of knowledge was how to avoid distorting the very same data that was being transferred. Human beings are keyed to applying mnemonic shortcuts to everything they see or hear in order to store it more easily. Over time, the accumulation of these necessary changes passed from individual to individual, creates a distortion that only deepens the more complex the data become.

(Diagrams in this chapter are courtesy of P. McCarthy).

Martial arts knowledge and lore are not exempt from these hurdles. In fact, their transmission has two added aspects that make them more difficult to secure their integrity.

1. On the one hand, teaching martial arts before the development of video images meant it was necessary to explain dynamic movement using nondynamic media. As a result, even the most detailed written description or pictographic image had a high probability of missing crucial aspects of the technique.

2. On the other hand, the sectarianism of the different schools of martial arts and the desire to keep a certain set of fighting movements secret meant that information needed to be encrypted in a manner that only members of the group could decipher it and eventually became the reason why so many techniques got such poetic names as "Snow gives way" or "Immortal leaves the cave."

Martial arts manuscripts were the solution adopted by the masters to preserve and transmit secret knowledge outside of their reduced group of direct disciples, and "Bubishi" is the name given to, arguably, the most famous of these manuscripts.

The Bubishi is an undated, anonymous document that compiles tactical and philosophical applications of fighting techniques derived from the Chinese martial tradition. It is actually not a single book but a set of different versions of a manual created by several fighting schools in the Okinawan archipelago.

There is consensus that the Bubishi as we know it today is the result of multiple authors, and its disjointed nature shows the hands of generations of contributors who sought to add and enhance the contents of the manuscript. The name itself is unassuming: the Japanese interpretation of the Chinese-written characters is simply "Martial Manual." The most prevalent theory about its origins is that Chinese exiles from the southern Fujian province arrived in the Okinawan archipelago and spread the practice of their native fighting styles, like White Crane, Monk Fist, and so on. The Bubishi was the outcome of different masters putting onto paper notes about their fighting lore. Senior students of each master would, in turn, copy the manuscript before setting out on their own. Over time, each new version would differ slightly from the source in order to match the particular preferences of the individual, and it is estimated that, at one point, over 20 different versions of the Bubishi existed in Okinawa.

The content is divided in sections and includes, among others, the following:

- Philosophy principles and social etiquette.
- Chinese medicine and herbal pharmacology.
- A summary of vital points (also called pressure points) in the human body.
- An explanation of fighting techniques.

The importance of the text lies in the view it provides of the historical development of martial arts. Okinawa has had a long fighting tradition and eventually became the cradle of karate, but before Gichin Fukakoshi, developer of the modern system of karate, wrote the first treatises in the 1920s, there were virtually no documents about the subject besides the surviving versions of the Bubishi. Funakoshi himself relied on the text and, acknowledging its value, included passages from it in his works.

Transmission of Knowledge in Martial Arts

When reading the Bubishi at some depth, there is one particular thing that stands out: over and over, the information that the authors present is conveyed as a set of principles of arcane knowledge, something that is both secret and mysterious. But what they often speak of seems fairly obvious to the modern reader: using movement to prevent attacks; targeting weak areas like the neck, eyes, or groin; or bending the joints to submit the opponent are all notions that appear self-evident. Even people who had never taken up martial arts or fighting training are aware of these, since many biomechanical principles are shared with other forms of physical activity and sports. Why the need, then, to collect them in a secret manuscript?

Modern citizens living in the age of communication are constantly exposed to information: movies, documentaries, and news stories are channels where the principles of fighting appear regularly, and even those not interested in the topic will have some understanding of how a punch is thrown or evaded. But that is a recent phenomenon, and, for centuries, the average person in the pre-industrial Far East was oblivious to concepts like biomechanics and the laws of physics applied to the human body. Related ideas like kinetics, kinematics, as well as the study of inertia, torque, and motion were not only unknown but so removed from their day-to-day experience as to be incogitable.

Furthermore, the basis of scientific thinking as the self-correcting and analytical process we are accustomed to now was not present at large during the time covered by the Bubishi, so the systematic and rational view it takes about the art of fighting in its pages was far above the consideration that any normal farmer or manual worker of its time may have had.

The masters of the Bubishi not only spent years studying and systematizing their first-hand experience about what worked and what did not when engaging in physical conflict but also had to solve the puzzle of how to transfer that information in a manner that was confidential and reliable.

Eventually, three paths of transmission appeared:

1. Direct contact. These were lessons in which teachers would host selected students (such as family members or properly introduced acquaintances) at their own homes. The teacher would impart lessons in exchange for remuneration or services, although martial arts practice was generally not considered a hobby or a sport but a serious, dedicated endeavor.

2. Forms or *kata*. These were prearranged sets of movement that represent a fight. Teachers would create the form so their disciples could learn and further transmit how to move during a confrontation and where and how they needed to use the different techniques. Forms were arranged in such an order that made them progressively more complex so that students could build on their own foundation of expertise. These forms acted as mnemonic systems, and teachers emphasized the need for accuracy when performing the moves to avoid deviation from the original movement map. An untended result of the creation of forms was that during the process that transformed karate from a free, intuitive, and rather loose set of fighting styles to a strict hierarchical

institution, there was a shift that focused on maintaining the corpus of knowledge rather than achieving true fighting prowess. This process, in turn, remodeled the forms or *kata* from being a tool to learn how to fight into an end in itself, where the actual performance of the *kata* was the desired result regardless of any practical application.

3. Written texts and manuscripts. These were written documents used to compile fighting knowledge. In the Bubishi, the final section, called Article 29, collects 48 images representing multiple fighting scenarios; one person attacks with a particular technique and another applies the appropriated response. The 48 self-defense diagrams are a treasure of knowledge not only for the detail they show about each particular technique but also for the strategic insights they impart.

Point 1 has limited application for the world of business, but from Points 2 and 3, several lessons can be observed.

Business Learnings from the Bubishi's Kata

One of the most defining characteristics of the Okinawan martial arts that would eventually become karate is the practice of solo drills called *kata*, where the karateka moves around punching, kicking, blocking, and parrying in a precise sequence.

Kata is mentioned continuously across the text as the basic training method and practice tool, one that provides multiple benefits, including the somewhat metaphysical concept of opening the breathing and energy passages of the human body, which are often clogged due to both "vice and inactivity."[1] From this perspective, *kata* is both a therapeutic and a moral practice, which involves a set of physical and mental aspects:

1. Physical aspects.
   a. Breathing: This is a way to eliminate distractions. Technically, correct breathing comes from keeping the spine parallel to the stomach in a two-tempo pattern: when inhaling, the body becomes light; when exhaling, it becomes rooted.

---

[1] P. McCarthy. 1995. "The Bible of Karate: Bubishi." Rutland, VT: Charles E. Tuttle.

    b. Balance: In the Bubishi, balance is "an external reflection of what is within and a prerequisite for combative proficiency." It relates to correct body posture and proper alignment from head to toe in order for hands and foot techniques to be delivered properly. A weakness in balance is an opening that a competent opponent can exploit.

    c. Movement: The principles of movement involve the combination of strength/firmness with mobility/pliability. The text gives some precise advice: "foot movement, both in a forward and backward direction[,] should correspond to the crescent shape of a quarter moon, with the knees slightly bent, moving quietly."

All three aspects are dependent of and related to each other; breathing has to be harmonized with movement even when walking, so that in the event of being suddenly attacked, balance is not lost.

2. Mental aspects.

    a. Introspection: Fang Qiniang, the mythical founder of one of the Chinese martial styles that appear in the Bubishi, White crane boxing, admonished the placing of too much emphasis on physical strength and noted that true power comes from within, as a result of both wisdom and a philosophical understanding of the fighting principles.

    b. Discipline: Discipline in martial arts practice translates into discipline when engaging an opponent. As a result, the Bubishi details, the mind will be calm but alert, the eyes will look for what is not easily seen, and the body will have a confident posture and facial expression.

    c. Patience. Karate training sought to imprint character in its practitioners by demanding full dedication and patience: "Study diligently two or three hours every day. After four years of unremitting effort one's body will undergo a great transformation, revealing the very essence of karate."

The three mental benefits of kata practice are also interrelated: introspection leads to self-understanding, which increases discipline. A disciplined mind controls itself and breeds patience.

It is easy to dismiss the physical and mental aspects of kata described in the Bubishi as either self-evident or impractically esoteric, but that would mean missing what its authors were trying to convey. In business, just as in martial arts or any other serious occupation, internal attitude and external action have to be harmonized. A successful mindset needs to translate into actions that are oriented toward success. A disciplined workflow can be put into practice only by a disciplined mentality.

In fact, this duality permeates every aspect of corporate behavior, even today. The strategic PDSA (plan-do-see-act) action flow is a planning and testing method commonly used in companies to develop new processes and to improve existing ones.

1. Plan: Create a theoretical blueprint.
2. Do: Apply the strategic plan into specific actions with limited scope.
3. See: Evaluate the result of the test.
4. Act: Roll out the new strategy based in the learnings of the previous three steps.

It is, at its core, the modern enterprise equivalent of the pairings of mental and physical actions described in *kata*.

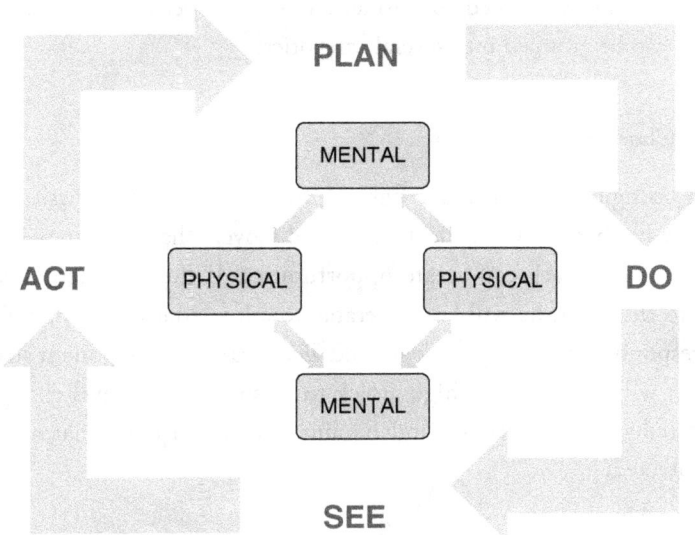

Business Learnings from the Bubishi's 48 Diagrams for Self-Defense

Among the most studied parts of the Bubishi are the 48 self-defense diagrams. The section, located near the end of the book, is given less space than the medicine chapters or the pressure point explanation, but these are the pages that, arguably, have given the Bubishi the cult-like status it has today.

The 48 diagrams for self-defense do not showcase complex martial arts techniques or flowery moves; the attacks are simple, direct, and often ruthless. But, above all, they are highly strategic, driving home the need for scientific thinking applied to physical confrontation and the understanding of body mechanics, distance, and timing.

Although they contain a wealth of fighting knowledge, the accuracy of the images and the actions performed by the figures has been diminished by the multiple reinterpretations of the text, while the names given to the techniques are purposefully obscure and ambiguous. Author and martial arts historian Patrick McCarthy has worked for decades in refining the understanding that can be gleamed from the original Bubishi[2] and has added explanations that go a long way in clarifying the moves of each illustration.

The strategic insights derived from the diagrams go beyond fighting and can easily be applied to business. From this perspective, the techniques can be grouped into several categories:

Level Change

Level changing is an advance fighting fundamental. Once basic competence has been developed, the fighter discovers that variations in the height of an attack can create opportunities. If the opponent strikes high to the head, he will be vulnerable to a low attack and the fighter can respond by targeting the legs. And vice versa, if the opponent strikes low, he will be open to a high attack to torso or head. Level changing helps reduce predictability, and its aim is to reach areas that are left unprotected.

---

[2] *Ibid.*

The business application seems obvious: rather than meeting force with force, be it in a negotiation setting or in other work situations, it is better to cover oneself up and then react by taking an action that uses a window of opportunity. This often requires a degree of creative thinking or an out-of-the-box approach in order to catch the opponent off balance. Planning capabilities are less relevant than reaction time and the ability to accurately read the movements of the adversary.

Informal styles, like the promoter or the supporter, will find this type of approach easier to apply due to their flexible nature and adaptability. Formal styles, like the controller or the analyst, on the other hand, may discover that it is harder to step out of the established processes they favor to apply the on-the-spot corrections that effective level-changing requires.

Diagram Number 3

When the fighter on the right tries to grab with both hands, the fighter on the left drops to the ground and applies a leg scissor technique.

WINNING TECHNIQUE
Dropping to the ground and capturing legs like scissors

LOSING TECHNIQUE
Trying to catch a fish by moving hands in the water

Diagram Number 10

When the fighter on the left attempts a takedown technique, the fighter on the right responds by striking the temples or slapping the ears.

白猴打等手敗

逆龍戲珠手勝

LOSING TECHNIQUE
White monkey breaking bamboo

WINNING TECHNIQUE
Twin dragons playing with a pearl

Feint and Deception

Fighting is not just a physical conflict; psychological advantages play a significant role, and a fight can change its flow depending on the wavering perception fighters have of themselves or their adversaries. It is not uncommon that a strong, sudden blow creates doubts in an otherwise-confident fighter and leads him to defeat.

Several techniques in the Bubishi refer to the importance of psychological combat with two different applications:

- As a way to appear weaker or inept in order to lure the opponent into a false sense of security.
- As a way to appear more threatening in order to discourage the opponent from attaching.

In a business environment, a clear translation of the second case into action is the use of legal written deterrents to stop competitors from acting in a certain manner. When these take the form of "cease and decease" letters, they may not have the ultimate intention of moving into a legal procedure but leverage the explicit threat of doing so to force the other party to give up. Even when lawsuits do happen, they can also be interpreted as posturing to scare competitors.

Out of the four behavioral styles, the promoter is certainly the most suited to apply this type of feint and deception techniques because of his or her emotional and bombastic communication preferences. It is intrinsic to the promoter's nature to project an image of invulnerability, which may deter others from engaging directly.

Diagram Number 16

The fighter on the left feigns intoxication, weakness, or cowardice and waits until the fighter on the right drops his guard to attack.

WINNING TECHNIQUE
Drunken arhat

LOSING TECHNIQUE
Single ji *hand*

Diagram Number 23

The fighter on the right intentionally leaves an opening in his guard to lure an attack from the fighter on the left. When this happens, it is easy for him to block and counter at will.

鉄牛入石手敗

鯉魚猷肚手勝

身燵手入

LOSING TECHNIQUE
Iron ox hits stone

WINNING TECHNIQUE
Catching ribs like a carp jumping out of the water

Weak Spot Targeting

This is a very recurrent theme in the 48 diagrams: no less than 10 of them show a fighter striking the eyes, groin, or neck of the opponent or pulling his hair to yank the head back. Although knowledge about these biological weak spots was hardly a martial secret, what the Bubishi shows in the illustrations is how to strategically select one target or another, depending on the opponent vector of attack and the fighter positioning, for maximum effectiveness.

The business application of these techniques relates to the somewhat merciless nature of corporate conflict, where any advantage a company may have over another is exploited without qualm. Weak spot targeting in a corporate setting requires a similar dehumanization of the adversary and will-to-win at any cost to the one presented in the legacy of the Bubishi's karate masters. Dumping prices to hurt competitors, forcing suppliers to reduce their margins, even internal processes that increase pressure on employees to secure the company's bottom line are all adaptations of these same principles.

While a profile like the analyst may lack the necessary drive, the controller, due to its formal leaning and proactive focus on efficiency, is well suited for weak spot targeting actions. The promoter and supporter may find them more difficult to apply due to their empathic nature.

Diagram Number 32

The fighter on the right attacks with a short punch, which the fighter on the left checks before responding with a strike to the eyes.

WINNING TECHNIQUE
Phoenix spreads its wings

LOSING TECHNIQUE
Dragon spits pearls

Diagram Number 33

The fighter on the left tries to grab, and the fighter on the right defends by striking the groin and grabbing the hair to throw his opponent to the ground.

LOSING TECHNIQUE
Qilin *(Chinese unicorn) opens*
its mouth to eat

WINNING TECHNIQUE
Golden lion shakes
its mane

As the science of fighting and the interest in historical martial arts increase, the contents of the Bubishi also continue to be studied and rediscovered. The text is far from being considered an austere relic of bygone eras but, rather, offers a vibrant window, through which two of the most human compulsions (the will to fight and the need to communicate) come together and are laid bare for study. As McCarthy quotes in his analysis:

> Through studying the past we are brought closer to understanding the present. My analysis of the Bubishi has had a profound effect upon not only my art, but upon my life in general. I hope that the glimpse of the past provided by the Bubishi and its profound teachings will have as positive an influence on you as they have on me, and that it has brought you closer to that which you have yet to discover.

CHAPTER 11

The Supporter Style

CEO Use Case: Satya Nadella, a Man of Empathy

When Satya Nadella took over the position of Microsoft's CEO in 2014, everybody was ready for a change. After all, he was succeeding Steve Ballmer, who, as the previous head of the company, had brought his brass personality to the job and was notoriously famous for his unorthodox public appearances. He often took to the stage while screaming, "I love this company!" and dancing around in a manner that was seen as excessive even by the outlandish standards of Silicon Valley.

But Nadella seemed a bit too much of a change for some; a quiet and unassuming long-time Microsoft employee, the most astonishing characteristic he had was that nobody seemed able to say anything bad about him. That was particularly relevant in a corporate culture as competitive as the one Bill Gates had developed in Microsoft for years and where everybody strived not only to be the smartest person in the room but also to show it.

From the get-go it was clear that Nadella was a team player and very adept at building personal connections. As a big fan of the sport of cricket, he knew that not a single person has all the answers and that the key to revitalizing the company was the same one needed to play that game: people had to work together. He went as far as recruiting an NFL sports psychologist to help his leadership team bond in a similar manner to that in which high-performance sport teams do.

For Nadella, communication is not just an abstract concept. His oft-quoted three rules of leadership are: (1) provide clarity, (2) generate excitement, and (3) make things happen, all of which require extraordinary engagement skills from a manager.

Nadella's focus on communication and empathy is evident in one of the anecdotes mentioned in his 2017 book *Hit Refresh: The Quest to Rediscover Microsoft's Soul and Imagine a Better Future for Everyone*, where he describes the scenic, all-expenses-paid retreats where senior members of the management team would gather from time to time:

> One aspect of the off-site really bugged me. Here we were with all this talent, all this bandwidth, and all this IQ in one place just talking at each other in the deep woods. And frankly it seems like most of the talking was about poking holes in each other's ideas. Enough. I figured it was time to hit refresh and experiment.

He changed the dynamic of the retreat by bringing in more junior, younger members, in order to break the exclusivity of membership and include new perspectives:

> These new Microsoft leaders were mission-oriented, innovative, born in the mobile-first and cloud-first world. I knew we could learn from their fresh, outside perspective. The only problem was that most of these leaders did not officially qualify to go to the executive retreat given the person's level in the organization. To make matters worse neither did the manager, or even the manager's manager. Remember, the retreat had been only for the most senior leaders. Inviting them was not one of my more popular decisions. But they showed up bright-eyed, completely ignorant of the history. They asked questions. They share their own journeys. They pushed us to be better.

No matter what the initial reaction was or how difficult changing the Microsoft corporate culture turned out to be, as a result of his new perspective, Nadella was responsible for turning around the fortunes of Microsoft, a very large corporation, which while still relevant, had been seen for years as outdated. He worked on developing a whole new host of cloud infrastructure and services that revitalized the company and increased the stock price over 130 percent by the time he was done.

Further than that, his success proved that the image of authoritarian leadership as an essential condition to run large corporations in a highly competitive environment is not necessarily correct. Both Nadella's behavioral type, which relies on cooperation, sincerity, and interdependability between team members, and his calm manner and calmer approach correspond to the most egalitarian of styles: the supporter.

The Bases of the Supporter Behavioral Style

The supporter is a sympathetic behavioral style that relies on personal connection and empathy. The supporter can be described as the "gregarious democrat," two words that summarize quite well this particular mindset.

- Gregarious because supporters like to engage in interpersonal communication; they are usually good listeners who focus on cooperation, sincerity, and being dependable.
- Democrat because they are sincere egalitarians, who often dismiss the most competitive aspects of corporate behavior and are, therefore, more willing to be of service to others.

Supporters in culture and media are often portrayed as the heart of the group; they are the characters who help maintain balance and create consensus so the plot moves ahead, deftly offsetting the abruptness of the controller or the remoteness of the analyst to bring the team together in the moments of crisis. This is the affable Porthos in the three musketeers, Ray Stantz (Dan Aykroyd) in Ghostbusters, or even Ringo Starr in the Beatles.

With a causal style and friendly manner, the supporter comes across as a very likable person. It is no surprise then that, within an organization, supporters often fill roles in human resources or those positions that require reconciling factions as well as applying a personal touch to inter-group problem-solving. The supporter has a higher-than-average sense of what the emotional motivators are that drive other people's actions and can apply a calm, dependable approach.

Taken to the extreme, the supporter behavioral style can come across as too consensual, when their tendency to avoid conflict results in a lack of assertiveness; they like to agree with the majority because it prevents them from upsetting others. In those cases, it is important for the supporter to realize that being a good team player and wanting to build positive relationships cannot come at any price. Because of their informal leanings, supporters can find trouble in an environment that lacks structure; they prosper better in a clear goal-setting system since, on their own, planning is neither a priority nor a strength.

The supporter style benefits from learning formal traits from both the controller and the analyst. Adding a proactive attitude will take them closer to the promoter style, which means increasing decisiveness while retaining that elusive quality that makes them come across as sincere in their personal interaction with others.

The Supporter at the Table: Negotiation and Communication Style

The supporter is the ultimate "people's person." This is a behavioral style that is at its best when engaging with others, and supporters make the best of this ability. Their inclination to be responsive rather than proactive means listening comes naturally, while their informal approach makes it easy for others to relate to them. Supporters excel at creating lasting relationships and developing close links that go beyond the work environment. Also, their empathy sets this as the most accepting of all four behavioral styles and can, with equal ease, build rapport with either the controller, the analyst, or the promoter.

From a communication perspective, supporters are unpretentious and do not try to impose their opinion on others, but this open disposition comes with two drawbacks:

1. The first one is a lack of urgency. Building relationships toward an objective takes time, and the supporter will happily subordinate this setup to the objective itself. Where a style like the controller is

results-driven, it could be said that the supporter is process-driven, similar to the analyst, but with a more human dimension, which can result in loss of focus or significant delays.

2. The second is, as the name indicates, an inclination to support, often putting others ahead of themselves and, as a result, falling short of their own objectives. Even when supporters see this happening, their empathic nature will not allow them to change priorities spontaneously.

The best way to engage with a supporter is by letting communication happen in a natural way. Rather than holding a meeting, simply getting together with him or her in a more informal setting (coffee or lunch) will achieve the same result and will feel more organic.

The Supporter at the Helm: Leadership Style

The supporter is a leader of consensus. Even if they have the power to implement decisions, supporters will often look for a way to make theirs palatable for the whole team. These are inclusive leaders, who find power by empowering others, and their personal skills mean they can get the best performance out of their subordinates not via pressure but by having them be invested in the larger goals.

One of the biggest advantages of the supporter leader is his or her willingness to include and accept opposite views from the team in the decision process. Supporters will often have members who can play devil's advocate and will listen to all opinions even if these clash with their own. A derived benefit of this is that the supporter's decisions carry a low risk factor because they are not based on a single perspective but rather on an amalgamation of inputs that, ideally, distills the best characteristics of all approaches.

When talking about the negative traits of the supporter leadership, the two main issues they encounter are:

- A tendency to become passive if consensus cannot be achieved because of their reluctance to enforce decisions from a top-down perspective.

- A tendency to be overly trusting at a personal level, with the corresponding risk of having subordinates undermining their authority.

The Supporter: Relationships Chart

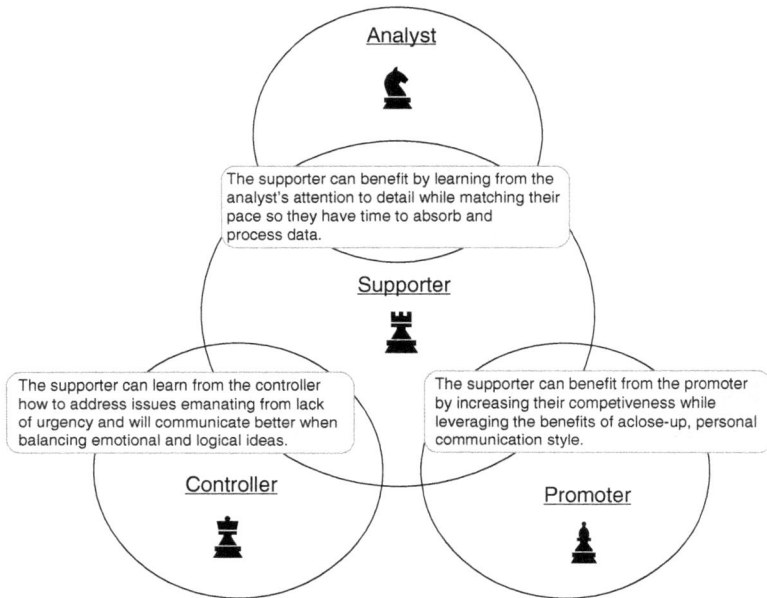

Analyst

The supporter can benefit by learning from the analyst's attention to detail while matching their pace so they have time to absorb and process data.

Supporter

The supporter can learn from the controller how to address issues emanating from lack of urgency and will communicate better when balancing emotional and logical ideas.

The supporter can benefit from the promoter by increasing their competiveness while leveraging the benefits of aclose-up, personal communication style.

Controller

Promoter

CHAPTER 12

Brazilian Jiu Jitsu (BJJ)

The Supporter Fighting Style

The Story of Brazilian Jiu Jitsu

When the doors of the now-defunct McNichols Sports Arena in Denver, Colorado, opened on November 12, 1993, the small pool of eight fighters who had agreed to compete that day and the attendance of less than 8,000 people who had gathered to see them do it had a clear objective in mind: to find out, once and for all, which fighting style was the most effective in a no-holds barred tournament.

For 40 odd years, since Western countries started to learn about Asian martial arts in the aftermath of World War II and judo, aikido, karate, kung fu, muay thai, and other styles became known to a global public, the great question many had put forward was, Which one is a superior, more effective fighting method? karate boasted great popularity, judo had the same plus some Olympic credentials, and boxing enjoyed the most solid commercial appeal, while aikido and kung fu held an aura of almost supernatural efficiency. But despite some previous attempts to pit one style against another, the rules and regulations governing competition for each were too dissimilar and gave an advantage to the specific martial art they were designed for.

That day in 1993, representatives of multiple fighting schools like savate, sumo, kickboxing, taekwondo, and boxing solved the issue by removing all rules except the most safety-related, basic ones. Aside from biting and eye gouging, everything else was permitted; grappling, striking, elbowing, kneeing, and head-butting were all fair play. There was no time limit for the matches, and they were to end only by knockout, submission, or if one of the fighters threw in the towel.

At the end of the night, none of the major, more popular martial arts styles came out on top. Instead, the representative of an obscure subset of judo that originated in Brazil was crowned as the world's Ultimate Fighter: Royce Gracie. Gracie's modus operandi was similar in all those initial fights: he would protect himself from punches and kicks while waiting for an opening, he would then shoot a take-down, grab his opponent, and drag him to the ground, where he would easily find a position of control and choke or submit at will. Gracie would go on winning for several more tournaments, and through him, the world discovered the art of Brazilian jiu jitsu (BJJ).

One of the reasons why BJJ proved so successful initially was that it arrived at a time when there was a general dismissiveness in the world of martial arts toward all grappling styles of fighting. It is true that judo and Greco-roman wrestling were both highly popular, but they were seen more as point-based sports. When it came to real fighting, the striking styles were considered much more effective, and standard wisdom held that a good punch or kick could stop any takedown attempt by a grappler. But as BJJ pioneer Carlos Machado said in an issue of *Black Belt Magazine* from 1994:

> After the clinch, it doesn't matter what happens, one way or another, we're going to hit the ground, and we'll be in my world. The ground is my ocean, I'm the shark, and most people don't even know how to swim.

The history of BJJ is closely linked to judo's founder, Jigoro Kano. After the initial success of judo in Japan, Kano understood the need to grow internationally, and in 1904, he sent one of his more advanced instructors, Mitsuyo Maeda, to the United States in order to spread the teaching of the new discipline. Maeda was a seasoned fighter even before studying judo, and during his tour in America and Europe, he accepted and won a large number of fighting challenges. Eventually, he settled in Brazil, where he opened a school that was known as Kano's jiu jitsu, using the name of the original discipline judo had emerged from.

Maeda's academy become popular and grew. One of his students was a man called Carlos Gracie, who eventually started his own training school. While judo in Japan was oriented toward the safer sport aspects of competition, Maeda's influence meant his jiu jitsu style, as the Gracie family received it, was more geared toward actual fighting efficiency. In order to keep the sense of urgency alive and avoid being constrained by potentially inefficient sport regulations, the Gracie students engaged regularly in open challenges, where they pit their art against other types of martial arts.

Another of the key difference between BJJ and its parent style of judo was developed by Helio Gracie, younger brother of Carlos. Of weaker constitution than his siblings, Helio was unable to perform many of the standing judo techniques taught by Maeda, so he focused on perfecting the ground-fighting aspects, where technical skill was more relevant than power or size. These highly specialized sets of moves are the stamp by which BJJ, in general, and the Gracie style, in particular, have become famous and represent a highly logical use of the fighter's stronger muscle groups against the opponent's weaker points, applied with minimal effort.

The Principles of Brazilian Jiu Jitsu

BJJ is, in summary, a wrestling fighting system similar to judo, from which it derives. The same as judo does, BJJ uses a set of techniques based on balance, leverage, and biomechanics. But where the former is rather strict in the form of these techniques, the Brazilian influence on BJJ has given it a strong sense of improvisation, flexibility, and personal customization that is not seen in the original style.

One of the premier BJJ world instructors and a renowned coach is the New Zealand-born John Danaher, who, in addition to a black belt from the Gracie school, holds a master's degree in philosophy from Columbia university and is often described as "BJJ's thinking man." Danaher describes the basis of BJJ as a four-step process, where the practitioner maneuvers to gain a dominant position and submit the opponent. The four-step approach is an excellent summary of what makes BJJ such an effective fighting style, simultaneously simple in conception and complex in execution.

Step 1: Take Your Opponent to the Ground

In a standing position, any person, even an untrained opponent, can push, punch, or kick abruptly. And because this is a natural stance for human beings, it allows them to instinctively generate a large amount of explosive power. Taking opponents to the ground removes their capability for unpredictable movement and reduces the number of angles from where they can hit back.

Step 2: Pass the Legs

Once the opponent is on the ground, the next step is to get through the obstacle that the legs represent. The legs have a larger amount of muscle mass than the arms, and an intuitive defensive reaction when lying on the back is to use them to kick up and front so they need to be neutralized quickly. BJJ has developed multiple techniques to get out from leg reach, pass the line of the hips, and safely move into a position near the head or torso.

As with Step 1, the objective is to reduce risk and uncertainty during the fight.

Step 3: Set a Dominant Position

Passing the legs is not enough to control the opponent because he is still free to rotate on his back and reposition himself. Now the objective is to secure a position from where the practitioner can hit or submit without the risk of being hit back. Some BJJ basic controlling positions ranked from lower to higher level of stability include the following:

- Knee on belly, where the practitioner stands over the prostrated opponent and controls him by pressing with one knee on the center of mass, usually the belly or lower abdomen.
- Mount, where the practitioner sits on top of the opponent's hips, one leg to each side. This position allows for control just using the legs, same as when riding on horseback, and leaves both hands open for attack or defense.
- Back mount, where the practitioner grabs the opponent's back and uses heels and hands to hold onto him. From back mount, he is safe from most strikes while being able to attack the neck and the head.

Step 4: Force a Submission

Setting a dominant position may be enough to hold the opponent (or make him submit using blows if such rules apply), but BJJ's trademark versatility relies on the wide range of submission techniques it has available. In order to finish the fight with maximal safety and minimal effort, the practitioner can either choke the opponent or apply arm or leg locks, putting pressure to the joints.

The four steps remain the same whether a BJJ practitioner faces an untrained opponent or another BJJ expert. In the second case, however, the fight becomes like a complex game of physical chess, where both fighters know the rules and need to trick or set up each other to find an opening and move from one stage to the next until reaching checkmate.

Brazilian Jiu Jitsu's Business Learnings for the Supporter

One of the most striking peculiarities of BJJ is how its Brazilian origins have given it a refreshing sense of informality, not common in the world of martial arts. Where other styles tend to be serious and strict in their manners, BJJ is not, and this becomes evident even in the nomenclature it has chosen. In judo, the original source of BJJ, sparring in free form is called *randori*. But that rather formal term was eventually substituted in the Brazilian incarnation of the art with the more friendly "rolling." Although BJJ sparring is highly demanding and intense, and its objective is to improve technique and performance by competing with a resistant opponent, it is very telling of the Brazilian influence that its practitioners selected a colloquial term that has connotations of relaxation and playfulness.

This informality is what makes BJJ sparring or rolling a rich ground where business learnings that align very well with the supporter behavioral style can be found. Some of them include the following:

Building upon Each Other

Taken at surface value, rolling resembles a wrestling match where two people grapple on the ground. But upon closer examination, it becomes clear that it is actually as close to a chess game as it is to a physical contest.

As in chess, one person cannot play alone, and reaching checkmate hinges upon finding and exploiting any error made by the opponent. A chess game is "a combination of moves where each playing piece is moved according to precise rules and the objective is to put the opponent's king under a direct attack from which escape is impossible," and it takes place in three stages:

- The opening, where players move from the initial starting places to take a central dominant position.
- The middle game, when both attacking and defensive moves happen.
- The endgame, when a combination of moves puts the king under attack and submission occurs.

Similarly, rolling in BJJ is a process where the players' collaboration in the frame of confrontation builds the match. Although a proficient practitioner could, in theory, apply submission to the perfectly defended, unmoving guard of the opponent, both players have to, in a sense, collaborate via attack and counter attach, move, and defense, until one gains a controlling position. In doing so, they teach each other what they should and should not be doing as well as what the holes in their game are.

Supporter behavior, even in a confrontational situation, is comparable to a BJJ rolling session and can learn to build upon others because it is, at its core, (a) collaborative and (b) communicative.

a) Collaborative because supporters do not do everything by themselves as the formal styles tend to but rather build upon the works of others and have others build upon their work in order to accomplish the task at hand.
b) Communicative because the supporter makes progress not by focusing on the task itself but rather by accomplishing the task through information exchange and personal contact with others.

Flowing and Staying Loose

The differences between BJJ rolling and sparring in any other martial art are noticeable from the onset; where judo or karate matches start with a formal bow, BJJ rolling partners slap their hands and bump their fists in an informal and friendly manner. The difference may seem trivial but it reflects strong conceptual distinctions between this particular style of fighting and the others discussed in this book. The relationship between practitioners is no less competitive or stringent but strives to establish a relaxed atmosphere, where those about to fight commit to keep the bout friendly, fair, and respectful.

BJJ fighters consider a fundamental condition for effective rolling is for it to be done in a relaxed manner, following a flowing pattern that allows the fighters to move seamlessly from one technique to another until finding the correct one from where to submit the opponent. As opposed to other sparring activities like boxing or karate, where the fighter can stay relaxed but still needs a certain degree of aggressiveness to prevail, in BJJ, rolling placidly can bring more wins than doing it harshly. In fact, it has some additional advantages: for one, rolling is a highly demanding physical activity and is usually set in standard 5-minute rounds. Doing it calmly, especially when facing more skillful fighters, helps conserve energy to go through several bouts. Being relaxed also allows the fighter to give up control of the fight; this does not mean letting the opponent control them but, rather, staying open to follow where the opponent may lead in order to exploit a gap. By giving up control, the mental pressure required to constantly maintain the initiative reduces, decreasing overall stress.

Similarly, the supporter can "roll" in a business environment using a relaxed approach and can work on developing a type of "antagonistic empathy" with his opponent in a constructive way so that at the end of the process, both have improved.

Using Frames and Levers

BJJ rolling emphasizes the use of the fighter's skeletal structure to move or push the opponent around, rather than relying on muscle power. By using frame-based movement, fighters can support their own weight as well as the weight the opponent throws on them without wasting energy, so a skilled BJJ practitioner will align the bones on arms and legs to use as levers and multiply the amount of force they use. BJJ black belt Rob Biernacki[1] describes this as follows:

> We want to use frames and levers against our opponent, and deny the use of them to our opponent. We seek to change frames into levers and levers into frames.
>
> When we combine this with an understanding of alignment, we can see that BJJ is the art and science of utilizing frames and levers to affect our opponent's base, posture, and structure, while maintaining our own. This leads to control, vulnerability, and ultimately submission.

If we consider the volume of marketing communication or business promotions as the raw "muscular" power necessary for a company to develop and sell a product or service, the supporter's biggest skill lies in developing personal contacts and close emotional relations. By treating such relations as a frame network, the supporter can develop an asset that goes a long way in supplementing expensive and time-consuming corporate processes and act as a lever to quickly expand business with minimal "muscular" effort.

Overlooked for almost a century, BJJ has gain deserved popularity in the last two decades as an effective fighting practice and has evolved from an overlooked status to the central stage in the martial arts ecosystem. Similarly, as evident in the increasing number of empathy-driven CEOs and managers the supporter behavioral style is becoming an untapped source of valuable leadership by doing what it does best: being humane.

---

[1] M. Mullen. 2016. Jiujitsutimes.com.

Conclusion

Business and fighting are, I believe, two sides of the same coin.

In 2001, when I began my professional career, I worked in Tokyo in a sales and consulting role. It was a results-driven environment, a high-pressure cookpot of an office that saw a high turnover of people. During a visit to one of my company's prospects, Mr. X, a formal, serious marketing director to whom I had been pitching our services for several months, remained peculiarly silent while looking at me carefully.

"I saw you on TV yesterday, Asensio-san. Fighting," he said finally.

I had started training in martial arts at age 13. It was originally a hobby that became more serious as I grew, and I spent my high school years obsessed over judo and moved later into other styles: boxing, kick-boxing, some poorly done kung fu. University found me fighting Saturday nights in cavernous sport halls and riding vans packed with other fighters to national tournaments with varying fortune. But fighting had never brought me any public recognition (aside from some small, forgotten article in the newspaper sport pages), so my surprise at Mr. X's comment was genuine.

I was, at the time, neck-deep in my Japan tournament years. After my share of amateur bouts and a successful national title run back home, I had qualified for the All Japan K2 full contact series, a championship popular enough to secure a cable TV appearance in the Greater Tokyo area.

For the next 20 minutes Mr. X, who had always stayed away from any even remotely personal topic, became animated and engaging for the first time since I had met him and asked me all manner of questions about the fighting world. As he spoke, I realized he was making this assumption, one that implied that some of the attributes of the fighter—at the very least endurance, grit, and perseverance—had to be present in my working ethos as well.

I don't remember if Mr. X's company ended up becoming a client of mine or not, but as my professional career developed, the episode stuck in my mind, and I started to see that more and more crossover between my martial arts training and my job was happening. Often, I would try to apply ideas from one to the other to solve problems and improve results.

It worked for me. It still does.

But then again, fighting is not for everybody, nor should it be. In my understanding, fighting is not about violence, that moment of nerve-wrecking confrontation with an opponent. It is about self-discovery: Who are you, when standing half naked with hands wrapped, under the brilliant lights of the ring, subject to the scrutiny of others?

Fighting can help you learn that, and for many, it does, but then again, so can painting, sailing, or music.

The objective of this book is not to convince people working in a corporate environment to sign up at the local gym and become white-collar boxers; neither is to recommend that they start practicing the particular martial art that has been associated here to their behavioral style. My hope is that the reading taken out of these pages is less literal but, perhaps, more relevant.

As Miyamoto Musashi put it, it is not about what you do but about how you do it: Do you have an attitude of sacrifice and perseverance? Do you apply a mindset of achievement to every task you are faced with? Do you labor to be better, to do better?

If you try, if you do, then for me, you are already a fighter.

A. Asensio. Tokyo, 2019

About the Author

Alfonso Asensio works as a Tokyo-based executive for a global technology company and has done extensive work in the field of data-driven marketing and digital advertisement.

A trilingual professional, he holds a master's degree from the Nagoya University of Japan, and his past work experience includes business roles with some of the largest Japanese consumer corporations. He has lectured as a professor of Asian Studies at the Madrid Chamber of Commerce in Spain and was guest speaker at the American Chamber of Commerce in Japan. He is a published fiction and business author.

He was a national kickboxing champion in Spain and a knockdown karate Japan silver medalist.

Index

OTHER TITLES IN THE HUMAN RESOURCE MANAGEMENT AND ORGANIZATIONAL BEHAVIOR COLLECTION

- *No Dumbing Down: A No-Nonsense Guide for CEOs on Organization Growth* by Karen D. Walker
- *From Behind the Desk to the Front of the Stage: How to Enhance Your Presentation Skills* by David Worsfold
- *The New World of Human Resources and Employment: How Artificial Intelligence and Process Redesign is Driving Dramatic Change* by Tony Miller
- *Our Glassrooms: Perceptiveness and Its Implications for Transformational Leadership* by Dhruva Trivedy
- *Virtual Vic: A Management Fable* by Laurence M. Rose
- *What Millennials Really Want From Work and Life* by Yuri Kruman
- *Temperatism, Volume II: Doing Good Through Business With a Social Conscience* by Carrie Foster
- *Practicing Management* by Alan S. Gutterman
- *Practicing Leadership* by Alan S. Gutterman
- *Women Leaders: The Power of Working Abroad* by Sapna Welsh and Caroline Kersten
- *Breakthrough: Career Strategies for Women's Success* by Saundra Stroope
- *Comparative Management Studies* by Alan S. Gutterman
- *Cross-Cultural Leadership Studies* by Alan S.Gutterman
- *No Cape Required: Empowering Abundant Leadership* by Bob Hughes and Helen Caton Hughes
- *Leading Organizational Transformation* by Linda Mattingly
- *Transforming the Next Generation Leaders* by Sattar Bawany

Announcing the Business Expert Press Digital Library

Concise e-books business students need for classroom and research

This book can also be purchased in an e-book collection by your library as

- *a one-time purchase,*
- *that is owned forever,*
- *allows for simultaneous readers,*
- *has no restrictions on printing, and*
- *can be downloaded as PDFs from within the library community.*

Our digital library collections are a great solution to beat the rising cost of textbooks. E-books can be loaded into their course management systems or onto students' e-book readers. The **Business Expert Press** digital libraries are very affordable, with no obligation to buy in future years. For more information, please visit **www.businessexpertpress.com/librarians**. To set up a trial in the United States, please email **sales@businessexpertpress.com**.